NATIONALISATION AND INDUSTRIAL CONFLICT

EXAMPLE OF BRITISH COAL-MINING

NATIONALISATION
AND
INDUSTRIAL CONFLICT

EXAMPLE OF BRITISH COAL-MINING

BY

S. K. SAXENA

THE HAGUE
MARTINUS NIJHOFF
1955

ISBN 978-94-011-8566-0 ISBN 978-94-011-9331-3 (eBook)
DOI 10.1007/978-94-011-9331-3

For my father

ACKNOWLEDGEMENTS

This book could not have been written without the help of a number of individuals and organisations. Prof. M. G. Levenbach read through the entire manuscript and offered useful suggestions. Prof. W. F. de Gaay Fortman made valuable criticisms on Chapters V and VI. The constructive remarks given by Dr. L. J. Zimmerman on Chapter I proved very useful. To all of them, I am extremely grateful.

In my field inquiry, I had the constant help of Mr. Gwyn Phillips. Without his assistance, I could not have collected the material needed for writing Chapter VI. The London offices of the National Coal Board and the National Union of Mineworkers were kind enough to allow me access to the necessary facts and figures.

I also wish to express my thanks to the Netherlands Universities Foundation for International Co-operation, The Hague, whose award of a fellowship enabled me to undertake this research and its publication.

S. K. SAXENA

Institute of Social Studies,
The Hague, The Netherlands,

February, 1955.

CONTENTS

CHAPTER I

THE GROWTH OF NATIONALISATION

In tracing the growth of nationalisation, we shall start by giving a brief historical survey of the foundations, assumptions and the gradual decline of the doctrine of *laissez-faire*. This will call for a brief description of the philosophical foundations on which the idea of *laissez-faire* rested. For, it must be remembered that the idea of a harmonious Natural Order and the respect attached to the institution of private property were the fundamental postulates around which the fabric of *laissez-faire* Economics was woven. Any extensive attempt in this direction will inevitably lead us far beyond the scope of our present work. We shall, therefore, give the barest outline of the views of important thinkers on (i) Natural Law and (ii) Private Property.

Foundations of laissez-faire:

Natural Law: "Awareness of the presence of a set of interrelated phenomena that give rise to 'problems'", writes Schumpeter, "is evidently the pre-requisite of all analytic effort. And in the case of social sciences, this awareness shaped itself in the concept of Natural Law"[1]. Natural Law has been defined as that "law which, grounded in the innermost nature of man or of society, is independent of convention, legislation or other institutional devices"[2]. It is held to be a set of rules of right or justice which is discoverable by every individual with the help of reason or of a moral sense. The authority of such a law rests

---

[1] *History of Economic Analysis*, (Ed.) E. B. Schumpeter, Allen & Unwin Ltd., 1954, p. 107.

[2] Gurvitch's article on "Natural Law" in the *Encyclopaedia of Social Sciences*, Vols. XI–XII, 1951 Reprint, p. 284.

in the Divine and is, therefore, superior to any laws ordained by human sovereigns. Most of the writers called it "natural" because to them it expressed the ideals which were "natural" to mankind, or were embedded in human nature. Different writers expressed the same idea in different ways. Grotius, the famous Dutch jurist, connected Natural Law with social instinct which all men possessed inherently in their natures. With Pufendorf, it revealed itself to man through reasoning based on experience. An "innate" moral sense, according to Hutcheson, showed men the rules of conduct. For the Physiocrats, it was a code of exact rules which could be discovered by reason as applied to the facts of experience about men and their social relations. For Adam Smith, the Natural Law manifested the sentiments of justice caused by the feelings of "sympathy" aroused in man by his connections with his fellow-beings. Despite these divergent views, there was a common philosophical method employed. The peculiarity of the philosophy of Natural Law is not that it seeks to derive a set of moral laws from the natural order of things, but "rather its attempt to *identify* 'is' and 'ought', the actual and the obligatory, directly and without lengthy proofs; it simply equates reason and nature"[1].

Private Property: A second concept which lies at the foundation of the doctrine of *laissez-faire* is the respect attached to private property. Since Hellenistic times down to the present day, theologists, political philosophers and jurists have all speculated on the desirability or otherwise of private property in society. Plato described two systems of property, one for the perfect state in his *Republic*, and the other for the more attainable form of society in his *Laws*. Plato showed himself to be a communist, but only a communist in the case of "Guardians" and "Auxiliaries", since riches are likely to spoil them. Hence, for them, "no one shall have any private property, unless it is absolutely necessary"[2]. In his later work, the *Laws*, Plato made concessions to the weaknesses of human nature. Each citizen was allowed to possess equal private property and through a number of rules of in-

[1] Gunnar Myrdal, *The Political Element in the Development of Economic Theory*, Routledge & Kegan Paul, 1953, p. 28.
[2] Plato, *Republic*, (Lindsay's translation), p. 116.

heritance, each citizen's share was to be maintained at an equal level.

Aristotle divided property into two classes; first, the property which is held by natural right and which is granted to man by nature for his sustenance; secondly, the property acquired by man through trade or other devices invented by him. Property, especially slaves, was necessary for the maintenance of the unit of family, and since the family was an essential unit of the State, Aristotle justified private property as necessary in a good state. Property, by stimulating labour and thrift, also promoted these good qualities. However, Aristotle condemned usury and detested the idea of making fortune by lending money on interest.

The speculations of Plato and Aristotle have provided the framework for the thinking of future writers on the subject of private property. The ideas of the Hellenistic philosophers, carried to Rome mainly by the Stoic school, became incorporated in Roman Law and thus profoundly affected the views of both medieval and modern writers on the subject. Cicero and Seneca in Roman times and the early Christian thinkers reached the same goal, if through different routes. St. Thomas Aquinas, in the thirteenth century, "came to think that property and the political authority which protected it were not necessary evils but natural and good"[1]. In the sixteenth century, Bodin went still further and suggested that the reason for the existence of the state was the protection of the rights of ownership.

To Grotius, every man at first had an equal right to the unappropriated things of the material world. God gave the world to be used by man in common. The only property man had was the consumable goods which he obtained for his immediate use. Wants were simple and few, but gradually men grew discontent with what they had, and the desire to acquire more resulted in feuds. Things were divided by a tacit or an express understanding; the earth was divided not only among nations, but also among families, and "the preservation of peace required the institution of private property"[2]. This division of property, according to Grotius, was not an infringement of the Law of

[1] Richard Schlatter, *Private Property: The History of an Idea*, Allen & Unwin Ltd., 1951, p. 48.
[2] *ibid.*, p. 128.

Nature. In very extreme cases, the law re-asserts itself and overcomes the rights of property[1]. He believed that the understanding for introducing private ownership existed before laws were promulgated to give effect to this agreement. When the government comes into existence, the rights of the individual to property, with certain modifications, are to be respected by the State. "Grotius's theory of property", writes Schlatter, "is, in the main, the theory of the natural rights school"[2].

An important thinker whose views we ought to examine is John Locke. His ideas on private property are contained in a short chapter in his *Two Treatises of Civil Government*. One of the purposes of Locke's work was to justify the fact and principles of the Glorious Revolution of 1688, and, by building up a theory of property, to set limits to the overwhelming power of the government. Locke's first Treatise is an attempt at demolishing the two royal principles of (i) Divine Right and (ii) the duty of Passive Obedience, as were propounded by Sir Robert Filmer in his book, *Patriarcha*, which was published in 1680[3]. In the second Treatise Locke is concerned with discovering a rational justification of his view of government which would limit the power of government and not interfere with the fundamental rights of man to his life, liberty and property.

Locke starts out by a consideration of man's primitive condition, which he calls the 'state of nature', and of the steps by which men have established civil societies. Locke does not agree with Hobbes that life in the state of nature is "solitary, poor, nasty, brutish and short". Hobbes argues that in the nature of man, there are three principal causes of quarrel, *viz.*, competition, diffidence and glory. He writes: "Hereby it is manifest, that during the time men live without a common power to keep them all in awe, they are in that condition which is called war; and such a war, as is of every man, against every man"[4]. Locke, on the contrary, believed that the state of nature and the state of

---

[1] James Bonar, *Philosophy and Political Economy*, Allen & Unwin Ltd., 1927, p. 73.

[2] *op. cit.*, p. 129.

[3] See Bertrand Russell, *A History of Western Philosophy*, Simon & Schuster, New York, 1945, pp. 617–623.

[4] Thomas Hobbes, *Leviathan*, (1651), (Ed.) Michael Oakeshott, Basil Blackwell, p. 82.

war "are as far distant as a state of peace, good-will, mutual assistance, and preservation, and a state of enmity, malice, violence, and mutual destruction, are one from another"[1]. Thus, "men living together according to reason, without a common superior on earth with authority to judge between them, is properly the state of nature"[2]. All men, without discrimination, have certain rights. These rights Locke calls Natural Rights. In the state of nature property is held in common in the sense that every one has the right to draw his sustenance from whatever nature offers. Man has a natural right to that with which he "mixes" the labour of his body, *i.e.*, to property[3]. When society is formed, the individuals have not to surrender these rights. Rather, these rights are projected into the new society and it becomes the duty of the government to protect the private property of individuals and thus ensure the continuance of an institution which is in keeping with the Law of Nature. Hence "the great and chief end of men's uniting into commonwealths, and putting themselves under government, is the preservation of their property"[4]. Locke thus propounded his Labour Theory of Property which was destined to occupy in course of time an important place in socialist thought and in the formation of the Labour Theory of Value.

Unlike Grotius, who justified property by its historical origins, Locke was more concerned with giving a philosophical basis of the right of private property. With Locke, "property .... is made to rest upon something more ultimate than positive enactments or agreement; it is something in the very nature of things"[5].

Hume urged the principle of utility and rejected all theories of formal right. The rules of justice are conventions, because experience teaches us that they are useful and promote happiness. Man is selfish by nature, but he also realises the good which comes out of respecting other peoples' rights. Though nature

---

[1] John Locke, *The Second Treatise of Civil Government and a Letter Concerning Toleration*, (Ed.) J. W. Gough, Basil Blackwell, p. 11.

[2] *ibid.*

[3] *ibid.*, pp. 14–26.

[4] *ibid.*, p. 62.

[5] Casimir J. Czajkowski, *The Theory of Private Property in John Locke's Political Philosophy*, Notre Dame, Indiana, 1941, p. 75.

is not liberal, man is capable of creating abundance through his labour. "Hence the ideas of property become necessary in all civil society"[1]. Hume differed from Locke and maintained that labour cannot be "mixed", except in a figurative sense and that once a man acquires property through his own labour, there is nothing to oblige his fellow-beings to respect his right to that property. In this sense, Hume argued, the laws of property are a convention which men obey because it is to their interests to do so.

The idea of Natural Law and the respect attached to private property exercised a profound influence on the course of economic thinking and provided the philosophical basis of *laissez-faire* Economics. This would be clear by a brief enumeration of the assumptions of *laissez-faire.*

Assumptions of Laissez-Faire:

The term *laissez-nous faire* is attributed to the merchant Legendre who used it while addressing Colbert sometime towards the end of the 17th century. But it is held that the term in its present meaning was first used by Marquis d'Argenson about 1751[2]. The term implies that the government should keep its hands away from economic affairs and leave them to the individuals. The first assumption on which *laissez-faire* rests is rooted in the supposed existence of a natural order, distinct from the state of nature, as much in physical as in social affairs, which should be allowed to grind its own course with the minimum of outside manipulation. Secondly, *laissez-faire* rests on the belief that the individual is the best judge of his own affairs, both in the production and consumption of commodities. The source of wealth is the individual's initiative which exploits natural resources and produces commodities in the society. Goaded constantly by the idea of maximising his profits and producing under conditions of free and perfect competition, individual initiative will have to burn at its brightest if a firm is to survive in the market. Economic efficiency becomes automatically ensured since the less efficient units would be driven out of existence by the more

---

[1] Hume, *Essays, Literary, Moral and Political*, 1870, p. 419.
[2] J. M. Keynes, *The End of Laissez-Faire*, London, 1926, p. 18.

intelligent producers. Both in production and consumption, there would be an ideal distribution of products. Each consumer would plan out his expenditure in a way that would yield him the maximum satisfaction. The higher price that a consumer would be prepared to pay over the other buyers would only reflect the greater intensity of his demand, and, therefore, greater satisfaction. Hence the price mechanism would tend to portion out the available stocks amongst the consumers in the best possible way. The element of consumers' demand as a stimulus to the production to produce the maximum came into increasing importance when the shift took place from the cost-of-production theory of value to the marginal utility theory of Jevons and the Austrian school. Impelled, thus, by the desire to maximise their profits, cautioned by the fear of the competing rivals in the market and functioning broadly under the framework of effective consumers' demand as shown in the different series of price offers, the production units under a *laissez-faire* system would at once strike the delicate balance where the economy would function for the good of both the producers and of the consumers and, therefore, of the society as a whole. Any collective enterprise that took upon itself the unwarranted duty of tampering with this efficient and self-adjusting mechanism was bound to lead to disaster. It would, first, have to take upon itself the impossible duty of telling the individual what is, and what is not good for him in economic matters. Secondly, a state enterprise will lack the invigorating element of individual initiative which is the sole propelling force of the economic system and without which it would soon decay[1].

The credit of introducing the idea of *laissez-faire* in economic thinking goes to the Physiocrats, a school which developed in France in the eighteenth century and whose chief exponents were Quesnay, the Marquis de Mirabeau, Turgot, and Dupont de Nemours. "The cornerstone of their policy", writes Marshall, "was obedience to nature"[2], and their economic theory was

[1] Mill writes: "All the facilities which a government enjoys of access to information; all the means which it possesses of remunerating, and therefore of commanding, the best available talent in the market — are not an equivalent for the one great disadvantage of an inferior interest in the result". *Principles of Political Economy*, Vol. II, p. 553, London, Parker, Son and Brown.

[2] *Principles of Economics*, Macmillan & Co. Ltd., London, 1952 Reprint, p. 625.

essentially an exposition of the Law of Nature in its economic bearing. The Law of Nature, which we have briefly discussed above, refers to the material facts of life tending beneficently towards the highest welfare of human beings. These laws are immutable, and though human beings may, through ignorance or perversity, deflect from them, there is nothing that can thwart the teleological propensity of nature running its course towards a beneficent end. The natural right of man consists in doing what is advantageous to him and for finding out what is best, "we should seek to be enlightened by reflection, judgment, and the calculations of self-interest"[1]. The natural laws of the social order are the conditions under which men must act in order to enhance their interests in society. These rules are no "arbitrary contrivances, but flow from the essential justice that secures to men their subsistence and their enjoyment of their possessions without detriment to others; without them there is no security of life or possessions"[2]. The goal of this propensity is to promote the human well-being, but since economics has to deal with the *ordre physique*, it can only aim at achieving the physical well-being of men. Sustentation of mankind, therefore, becomes the primary objective of economics. Thus, agriculture alone is productive and has the character of economic substantiality. The whole question of value to the Physiocrats, therefore, is, as Veblen observes, "a question of the extent to which the given item of wealth forwards the end of nature's unfolding process. It is valuable, intrinsically and really, in so far as it avails the great work which nature has in hand"[3]. Agriculture alone being productive, its products should be allowed to be exported freely without any restraints. Free Trade with the Physiocrats thus became one of the natural laws of the social order. They justified the existence of private property and preached that the functions of the state should be limited merely to the maintenance of law and order and the protection of property. Any governmental interference in economic activities was an infringement of the natural order of things and, therefore, harmful.

[1] Bonar, *op. cit.*, p. 140.
[2] *ibid.*, pp. 140–41.
[3] *The Place of Science in Modern Civilisation*, New York, B. W. Huebsch, 1919, see the essay on "The Preconceptions of Economic Science I", p. 92.

Viewed against the background of the economic conditions of France when, under the influence of Mercantilism, numerous state decrees[1] had stifled the growth of the industries, the Physiocrats' insistence on *laissez-faire* looked like a reaction that flung the doors wide open to let the industries breathe freely without external restraints. It is not difficult to pick out faults in the ideas of the Physiocrats[2], but they are not relevant for our purpose. Suffice it to say that their work, though of little direct value, reflected a sustained effort at presenting an integrated picture of the economic system as a whole, an attempt at analysing the laws that made the economic system move. They derived their preconceptions from, what may be called, the "commonsense metaphysics of the eighteenth century, especially so far as concerns the enlightened French community"[3].

Adam Smith was influenced by the Roman *jus naturale* which came to him through Grotius and Pufendorf, while the more immediate influence on his thinking was derived from Locke, Hume, Hutcheson and the optimistic theism of the Scotch Philosophers[4]. Smith based his systems of ethics and economics on a harmonious order of nature which manifests itself through the instincts of the individual. Though in the *Theory of Moral Sentiments*, his earlier work, there is no clear formulation of the doctrine of *laissez-faire*, nor any express condemnation of governmental interference, it is pretty clear that Smith had already become the exponent of a system of Natural Liberty.

Smith argued that the beneficent order of Nature should be allowed to unfold itself in a system of Natural Liberty. Thus he writes:

---

[1] For some examples, see, C. W. Cole, *Colbert and a Century of French Mercantilism*, Vol. II, Columbia University Press, 1939, especially pp. 377–381. Also, by the same author, *French Mercantilism*, 1683–1700, 1943, especially Chapter III.

[2] For example, Marshall writes: "They confused the ethical principle of conformity to Nature, which is expressed in the imperative mood, and prescribes certain laws of action, with those causal laws which science discovers by interrogating Nature, and which are indicative mood". *op. cit.*, p. 626.

[3] Veblen, *op. cit.*, p. 95.

[4] *Adam Smith*, 1776–1926, (Ed.) J. M. Clark, Chicago, University of Chicago Press; Chap. V, Jacob Viner's essay on "Adam Smith and *Laissez-Faire*", pp. 116–155.

> All systems, either of preference or of restraint being thus completely taken away, the obvious and simple system of natural liberty establishes itself of its own accord. Every man, as long as he does not violate the laws of justice, is left perfectly free to pursue his own interest his own way, and to bring both his industry and capital into competition with those of any other man, or order of men[1].

The doctrine of free trade, which had been propounded by the Physiocrats, was so persuasively advocated by Smith that it became a great force in practical economic life. He limited the functions of the government to :(i) Protection of the society from external attacks; (ii) Establishment of an exact administration; and (iii) Erection and maintenance of certain public works. The protection of property was another duty of the civil government. Basically, the limitation of the government's tasks sprang, as we have already said, from his philosophical belief in the guiding hand of Nature. But, in addition, a number of objective factors also added to his mistrust of governments' efficiency in handling economic matters. The government, as Viner says, "was in the hands of an aristocratic clique, the place-jobbing, corrupt, cynical, and class-biased flower of the British gentry, who clung to the traditional mercantilism not so much because of a strong faith that it met the problems of a growing trade struggling to burst its fetters, but because they did not know anything else to do"[2].

Despite his ardent advocacy of *laissez-faire*, Smith was no dogmatic believer in its efficacy. He threw his net wide and his eclecticism made him approach every problem from diverse angles. He recognised that the economic order, when left to its natural course, gives rise to serious conflicts between the different sections of the community[3]. He also made exceptions to government non-intervention in the case of usury and Navigation Acts. But these exceptions are of minor importance and have hardly any

---

[1] Adam Smith, *An Inquiry into the Nature and Causes of the Wealth of Nations*, Edinburgh, Thomas Nelson, p. 286.

[2] *op. cit.*, p. 142.

[3] For example, writing on the "Wages of Labour", Smith observes: "What are the common wages of labour, depends everywhere upon the contract usually made between those two parties, whose interests are by no means the same. The workmen desire to get as much, the masters to give as little, as possible. The former are disposed to combine in order to raise, the latter in order to lower, the wages of labour". *Op. cit.*, p. 27.

significant place in his optimistic belief in the majestic natural order which grinds its own course towards human welfare. The doctrine of *laissez-faire*, destined to play a supremely important role in the realm of economic thinking, had found in Smith its most persuasive and systematic exponent.

From its inception at the times of the Physiocrats till the period when the Classical School held sway in England, the followers of *laissez-faire* formed a host of impressive economic thinkers. The central framework of economic theory had been woven round the writings of Smith, Ricardo and Mill. But the quick and successive victories won by the doctrine of non-interference in the realm of economic thought were also helped by a number of external factors. First, the advent of Industrial Revolution had made England the workshop of the world. The achievements of private enterprise were too glaring to be overlooked, and those of state-enterprise were hardly encouraging. Around the bustle of economic activity echoed the tremendous vitality of private initiative. The revolutionary changes in technical knowledge had given an exhilarating sense of increasing mastery over nature. What more proof could the man in the street have needed in support of the efficacy of privately run industry than the rapid strides made in the production levels with the coming of the Industrial Revolution, the continued flow of goods from factories which helped to raise the standard of living of the people.

Secondly, the philosophical teachings of Utilitarianism, a stream of thought which dominated the England of the 19th century, greatly strengthened the moral and ethical foundations of *laissez-faire*. Its chief exponents were Bentham, James Mill and John Stuart Mill. Its diverse ramifications, which reached into different branches of knowledge, — economics, politics, jurisprudence, penology, education and religion — were woven round the central principle of "the greatest good of the greatest number". "Nature has placed mankind", wrote Bentham, "under the governance of two sovereign masters, pain and pleasure. It is for them alone to point out what we ought to do, as well as to determine what we shall do". These pleasures and pains, which are experienced by all individuals can be reckoned in a hedonistic calculus. The principle of utility and the idea that the pursuit of self-interest without any outside interference will promote the happiness of the greatest number admirably suited the rising class of industrialists in England. They found in it the weapon with which to achieve the double aim of curbing the power of landed aristocracy and of enhancing their own. In short, by insisting that no rational grounds existed for preferring the happiness of one individual as against another, Utilitarianism emphasized the "greatest good of the greatest number" principle, a wish that *laissez-faire* claimed to fulfil; by regarding pleasure as quantitative, and social welfare as the aggregated welfare of all individuals in society, it neatly corroborated the harmony which, adherents of *laissez-faire* thought, existed between the interests of the individual and society.

Criticisms of Laissez-Faire:

Theoretical Objections: A little reflection will soon reveal that most of the assumptions on which *laissez-faire* rested were not as unerring as their advocates had thought them to be. We may first present some of the important theoretical criticisms. The consumers' demand, as reflected in the prices offered in the market, was supposed to be the guiding force that directed production along proper lines and also implied that the consumers were maximising their satisfactions. This did not take into account the inequalities in the distribution of wealth and thus ignored the cardinal fact that the same purchase price offered by two consumers with unequal incomes might represent differing degrees of satisfaction and urgency. The principle of "the greatest good of the greatest number" could have been promoted by a different pattern of distribution of income which would have resulted in a quite different series of price offers. As Cole says: "Price-offers in the market represent not proportionate lumps of expected satisfaction, or of desire, but only lumps of desire weighted in accordance with the size of the offerer's income and capacity for being satisfied"[1]. Furthermore, the adherents of *laissez-faire* had not implied that each individual was made best-off by competition, since, clearly, the best

[1] G. D. H. Cole, *Principles of Economic Planning*, Macmillan & Co. Ltd., London, 1935, p. 89.

possible position would have been when each individual could have all. This being obviously impossible, it was suggested that competition somehow maximized the sum total of individual satisfactions. Any such argument is bound to involve inter-personal comparisons of utility which will lead to highly subjective valuations and, therefore, cannot be subjected to scientific analysis. Moreover the theory of *laissez-faire* is incomplete. It takes into account only the goods and services enjoyed and ignores the disutilities caused by foregoing the alternative goods and services. Any theory with a claim for completeness ought to reckon both the positive and the negative magnitudes. In the liberal analysis, the work rendered and its distribution were taken as constant, because its inclusion would have brought the *laissez-faire* economists face to face with the difficulty of devising a measuring rod for estimating the disutilities[1].

Secondly, the state of pure competition envisaged by the *laissez-faire* economists was a myth. In reality, perfect competition with its full mobility of labour and capital, with its consumers' sovereignty and with its automatic efficient regulation of economic life, has never existed. Even the freedom of contract presupposes a certain number of rules and regulations to make this freedom an actuality. These rules and regulations profoundly affect price formations and thus infringe the assumptions of perfect competition. Seen in this light, the onus of proof does not lie only on the advocates of interference, as was preached time and again by the adherents of *laissez-faire*[2], but partly on those who refute it, if only to show as to what extent a measure of intervention leads us askew from the ideal state of perfect competition.

Thirdly, endowed with a certain quantity of goods and faced with a market situation, the equilibrium position reached under perfect competition represents an optimum for each individual. But that optimum may not necessarily be the best. What it amounts to is the fact that in a given situation the buyers and

---

[1] Myrdal, *op. cit.*, p. 135.

[2] See, for example, J. S. Mill, *op. cit.* After setting out the reasons why the state should not interfere, he writes: "few will dispute the more than sufficiency of these reasons, to throw, in every instance, the burthen of making out a strong case, not on those who resist, but on those who recommend, government interference", p. 556.

sellers are doing their best. But, then, it is quite possible to imagine a situation, other than pure competition, which may yield better results. "Is it not equally clear", asks Samuelson, "that under (say) monopoly, both buyer and seller are doing the best that they can for themselves under existing market situations"[1].

Facts against Theory: In course of time, as trade and industry expanded, the working of the doctrine resulted in unbalanced development of the economic mechanism and signs of chronic maladjustments soon convinced the economists that *laissez-faire*, despite its spectacular achievements in its hey-day, had to be seriously modified if a well-functioning economic system were to be evolved. By the middle of the 19th century, the achievements of the Industrial Revolution had also brought into existence facts which seemed to give the lie to the postulates of *laissez-faire*. The community, far from developing in a peaceful way, witnessed serious class struggles and "instead of the hoped-for harmony, a terrible antagonism had sprung up: the antagonism between factory-owners and factory-hands, between the lucky heirs and the unlucky disinherited, between capital and labour . . ."[2].

The whole course of the Industrial Revolution is a witness to the growth of the rising class of capitalists and a large army of industrial workers. Increasing industrialisation called for man-power and a great shift of population took place from rural to the new industrial towns. This class of proletariat swelled with frightening rapidity and soon an industrial reserve army stood by, ready to weigh down upon the wages of the workers in case the employed workers showed any signs of discontent. Lack of trade union organisation and non-recognition of the workers' rights left the proletariat in a miserable condition. The newer techniques of production and the expanding limits of the markets resulted in greatly enriching the class of industrial owners, but the workers, handicapped by the above-mentioned

---

[1] *Foundations of Economic Analysis*, Cambridge, Harvard University Press, 1948, p. 204.

[2] W. Stark, *The Ideal Foundations of Economic Thought*, London, Routledge & Kegan Paul Ltd., 1948, p. 149.

factors, sunk down to a low level. The impressive façade of the high peaks of production reached during the course of industrial revolution concealed a vast area of human misery and squalor[1]. Despite a few notable exceptions who illumined the dreary scene, Robert Owen for example, the general contours of the picture were hardly promising. Economic analysis, particularly value-analysis, under the rationalistic presuppositions of the eighteenth century, had come to be linked up ever more to the market phenomena and "Political Economy" had become "Economics". Money costs and returns dominated the thinking of economists and any factor lying outside the boundaries of the market became a foreign element to them, irrelevant for their purposes. The few crests of wealth amidst an ocean of poverty presented targets for attack by the social reformers, who considered the economic system to be immoral and based on a selfish philosophy. But in addition to this, from the economic angle too, the increasing pauperism of the masses created in course of time serious maladjustments, which received particular significance after traditional economic theory had witnessed spectacular developments. Moreover, the advance made in the electoral franchise — a political revolution which seemed to have been overshadowed by its more spectacular contemporary, the Industrial Revolution, but which was no less significant — had placed in the hands of the consumers an increasing political power which, they demanded, should be applied to more positive economic ends.

The maldistribution of wealth at which we have hinted in the above paragraph also considerably weakened the force of the consumer's sovereignty argument. The *laissez-faire* economists had assumed that the consumer, being the best judge of his own needs, knew what to pick from the market, thus directing production along the most desirable lines. In addition to the cases in which the individual cannot be the best judge of

---

[1] See, Marshall, *op. cit.*, p. 621: "Now first are we getting to understand the extent to which the capitalist employer, untrained to his new duties, was tempted to subordinate the wellbeing of his workpeople to his own desire for gain; now first are we learning the importance of insisting that the rich have duties as well as rights in their individual and in their collective capacity; now first is the economic problem of the new age showing itself to us as it really is".

his own needs and to which Mill has drawn our attention[1], there were other conditioning factors which seriously constricted the consumer's sovereignty in practical life. First, his low income was a restricting factor. The absence of strong trade unions in the earlier phase of the Industrial Revolution worked as a handicap. Secondly, advertising — a later phenomenon — began to modify the course of his demand, specially in the case of commodities which had an elastic demand. This is not to doubt the fact that the range of choice which the consumers enjoyed was wider than what they had, say, before the advent of the Industrial Revolution[2]. But the fact remains that in actual practice, the unorganized consumer was unable to influence the course of production, at least not to the extent which was envisaged by the *laissez-faire* economists. Moreover, *laissez-faire* took into account only the effective demand, and not the demand which was unbacked by the means for satisfying it. This fact had been hinted at by Smith and mentioned by Sismondi. But the credit of clearly formulating it goes to Rodbertus who showed that production by adapting itself to effective demand really meant that only those persons who already possess something are able to satisfy their wants[3].

Connected with the above is another evil of *laissez-faire*, the problem of unemployment. Prof. Carr says:

> Historically speaking, it was neither the need to mitigate the struggle between capital and labour nor the need to protect the consumer which drove the last nail into the coffin of *laissez-faire* Capitalism and provoked massive state intervention in every function of the economy. This was brought about by the problem of mass unemployment[4].

Unemployment in a *laissez-faire* economy is not a chance

[1] *op. cit.*, Bk. V, Chap. XI.

[2] On this aspect, see, *Capitalism and the Historians*, (Ed.) F. A. Hayek, Routledge & Kegan Paul Ltd., 1954. Ashton's essay on "The Standard of Life of the Workers in England, 1790–1830", pp. 127–159.

[3] Gide & Rist, *A History of Economic Doctrines*, Harrap & Co. Ltd., 1949, p. 421.

Also, Myrdal, *op. cit.*, "We are interested not only in the technical aspects of production, not only in how owners of productive factors dispose of them, but also in what kind of production it is, quite apart from the exchange value of the products; we are interested in how people work and in their welfare as producers", p. 136.

[4] *The New Society*, Lecture 2, London, Macmillan & Co. Ltd., 1951, p. 27.

phenomenon, but is bound up with the system itself. Shorn of its refinements, the process goes on like this. Once the effective demand goes down, the equipments lie idle and working hands are rendered superfluous. The level of investment goes down and along with it slump conditions set in, and conversely, a burst of investment generates a boom. These alternating waves of booms and slumps that wash up and down make the economic system unstable. The worst example of this tendency was witnessed during the depression of the inter-war years when the capitalists found it difficult to keep up the level of investment. These depressions, which were considered by the *laissez-faire* economists as temporary and minor aberrations from the general well-functioning of the economic system, assumed a different meaning when the slump of the thirties lasted for a number of years and when the staunchest supporters of *laissez-faire* began to feel that the economic system had seriously gone out of gear. It would have been the height of economic folly on the part of governments to have waited for the automatic adjustment of the system. In a number of countries the Governments intervened to remedy the malady through direct and positive action. But though these new conditions stimulated new approaches in economic theory, there was no theoretical tool in existence to show the way out of depressions and avoid mass unemployment. Neo-classicism dominated economic thought. Smith's "invisible hand" had been clothed in an intricate system of Marshallian equilibriums. Keynes's *General Theory* supplied this tool. Instead of starting from cost-price-profit analysis of individual economic units, Keynes considered the aggregate flow of national income as the main tool of economic analysis. He demonstrated that insufficiency of aggregate demand generates depression and unemployment, and showed that a position of equilibrium could be reached at a low level of economic activity. In the realm of economic policy, Keynesian findings provided a powerful justification for deficit financing by governments during periods of depressions.

A further assumption of *laissez-faire* was that the manufacturers and traders under perfect competition traded freely without any combinations. No individual producer produced such a large share of the total output that he could, by his own independent action, materially affect the price level in the market. But facts soon gave the lie to this assumption. The small competing units realized the dangers inherent in ruthless competition. Competition, originally thought of as a purge that would expel the inefficient elements, became a lesson which pointed towards combining the rival elements. In course of time, finding that this tendency towards concentration was inevitable, the supporters of *laissez-faire*, paradoxically enough, found themselves seeking state protection from outside interference in the affairs of these ever-growing organisations. The revolutionary advances made in technical knowledge and the growth of a world economy saw these organisations joining hands across national frontiers. Unhealthy rebates, restrictive policies in production and embargoes on new competitors became the watchwords of these monopolies. The liberal economists had not envisaged the practical possibility that profits could be maximised, not only by increasing production, but also, under monopolistic conditions, by curtailing it and thus raising prices. Repeated attempts at breaking the monopoly power of organisations in Germany and United States met with little success and each time the corporations deftly designed new garments for covering their old forms. It became evident that the state had to step in if the further excesses of monopolies were to be ended.

In addition, a number of other considerations favour the increase in the size of the firms. A complex splitting up of the processes of production calls for the installation of elaborate machinery. This entails large investments which a small organisation may not be able to obtain. Economies of bulk buying, creation and maintenance of specialized selling departments, the need for large funds and the acquisition of the finest entrepreneurial ability available are some of the factors which tend to enlarge the size of the organisations.

Another factor which undermined the faith in *laissez-faire* was the advent of World War I. The need for mobilizing the nation's resources to a single purpose with the minimum of waste and on an emergency footing showed the impossibility of achieving it in a fully privately run economy. An economy which ambled along at an easy pace and which, by a process of trial and error, tried to adjust itself to the whimsical forces of demand and supply, was the last thing suited for the feverish climate of wartime, when a central guiding control was essential for the successful prosecution of the war. From the consumers' point of view, it became necessary that the shortage of goods caused by the rupture of the distributive machinery under the stress of war should be spread out evenly in the society. Rationing schemes, price controls and quota systems marked the intervention of the state in a domain that was considered peculiarly suited for private enterprise by *laissez-faire* economists. Sometimes this was done by governments in collaboration with the consumers' cooperative movement. But a more important advance was caused by the overriding need for building up a wartime economy. In Britain, for example, immediately after the declaration of war, railways were taken over by the state. The motive that prompted this act was the efficient working of the railways for the movement of troops and other military requirements. In doing so, some drastic changes were initiated, which apparently would have been difficult if the railways had been operated under a system of private enterprise[1]. Even though in some cases the governments withdrew their control after the war, there was one thing which had been made abundantly clear, *viz.*, the indivisible nature of the national economy. In the meantime the Russian Revolution of 1917 with its emphasis on centralized control and direction of economic affairs caught the eyes of the world. The Five Year Plans in Russia, which in course of time had welded a highly divergent into an integrated economy, were the first systematic attempts at a practical demonstration of the efficacy of economic planning, and though some other countries decided to maintain a respectable difference of degree in government control, there emerged a distinct trend in the direction of conscious and deliberate control of economic forces. It became clear that unless the State exercised control over the main switches on the economic board, planning with the aim of attaining a certain rate of growth in one direction would be

---

[1] For a description of the extent of government control during wartime in Britain and the United States, see, Charles Whiting Baker, *Government Control and Operation of Industry in Great Britain and the United States during the World War*, (Carnegie Endowment for International Peace, Division of Economics and History: Preliminary Economic Studies of the War No. 18), New York, Oxford University Press, 1921.

difficult. The argument applied with still greater force in the case of public utilities and other basic industries. Sometimes considerations of technical improvement needed a layout far too extensive for the private enterprisers; often the relatively high proportion of fixed costs made competition wasteful. Sometimes small scattered firms had to be amalgamated into bigger units for the purpose of securing both external and internal economies. The desire for profits, severe competiton resulting in waste of economic resources, and the absence of a central body which could collect and disseminate knowledge about conditions affecting trade and commerce — since each individual entrepreneur was generally interested in having a partial view of the entire market — showed the incompatibility of planning and *laissez-faire*. It had become important for the successful execution of plans and for the smooth functioning of the economic system that the government should exercise a co-ordinated and intelligent judgment on savings and investments rather than leave them to private decisions and also maintain a certain level of economic activity by spending on items that were technically social, such as public works.

Approaches to Nationalisation:

So far we have given a brief historical survey of the gradual decline of the idea of *laissez-faire*. It is not within the purview of our subject to dilate upon the relative merits and demerits of Free and Planned economic systems. Nor is it relevant for our purpose to demonstrate whether a fully planned economy is consistent with rational economic calculation or not[1]. The term "nationalisation" is used loosely to indicate ownership or control by the state, but, strictly speaking, covers both, and it is possible for nationalised industries to exist in both types of economies. Broadly speaking, advocates of nationalisation can be classified as: (i) Non-socialists and (ii) Socialists. This classification, which seems to be customary among writers on nationalisation, is not to be interpreted in any rigid way. Oftentimes, a number of arguments find supporters in both camps. There are also differences among the same group about the way in which

[1] On this aspect see, *A Survey of Contemporary Economics*, Vol. I, (Ed.) H. S. Ellis, Richard D. Irwin, Inc., Illinois, 1952, Chapter XII, "Socialist Economics" by Abram Bergson.

nationalised industries should be run. We will now briefly present these two approaches.

Non-Socialists: To the non-socialists, nationalisation is a matter of expediency, and not of principle. Each measure of nationalisation is, therefore, to be justified on its own merits, *i.e.*, it should be conducive to the more efficient utilization of the limited economic resources of the society. Apart from the idea of enhancing economic efficiency, there might be a number of other factors which may point the way to nationalisation. An industry may be nationalised for the purpose of collection of revenue. Sometimes the production of articles of strategic importance is taken over by the state in order to ensure the military security of the nation. In economically backward areas where private capital is unable or unwilling to undertake developmental projects, the state may start industries on its own initiative. A last motive, also shared by the socialists, springs from the rather vague idea of promoting national interests. It might mean, as in the case of the depression period, the starting of new public works in order to infuse counter-cyclical movements in the economy. It can also be inspired by the desire to control the excesses of private monopolies, or, conversely, by the idea of creating a state-managed monopoly to achieve the desired economic efficiency.

Socialists: Towards the end of the 19th century the ideas of the Socialists began to acquire a more concrete form. Since then nationalisation of basic industries has figured on the programmes of the Socialist parties. But differences have existed as to the extent and speed of the change in ownership of industries. The Revolutionaries, deriving their inspiration from the Communist Manifesto, have advocated the idea of a wholesale change in ownership of the important industries. Piece-meal measures of nationalisation, according to them, are not only useless but definitely harmful, since they will only strengthen the hands of the Capitalist state and thus provide an obstacle to the achievement of the classeless society. The Evolutionaries, on the other hand, believe in the important role which the State can play in successfully nationalising industries in a peaceful manner. A second difference between the two broad groups of Socialists arises on the payment of compensation to the former owners of a nationalised industry. The Revolutionaries argue that industries ought to be nationalised without the payment of compensation while the Evolutionaries believe in reasonably compensating the expropriated owners.

But nowhere were the differences more marked than in the methods of control of industries as advocated by the different groups of socialists. The Revolutionaries themselves were divided on this point. To the orthodox Marxian, the nationalised industries were to be in the hands of the State which would be run by the elite of the Revolution immediately after it had taken place. Another branch, which for a time dominated the French labour movement, was Syndicalism. The Syndicalists believed that the new society could be attained through revolutionary trade unionism which, by the weapon of General Strike, could paralyze the capitalist society. They saw in the trade union the organ of government of new society. Control of the industries was to rest in the hands of the producers who would be formed in *syndicats*, which would be affiliated to the appropriate local and national organisations.

The State Socialists, on the other hand, believed that any scheme which sought to place the control of industries in the hands of the workers would result in inefficiency. They, therefore, recommended that nationalised industries should be run by the State through impartial and expert officials. The growth of the large-scale industry and the great amount of skill required in running it efficiently strengthened the arguments of the State Socialists. The post-war nationalisation programmes of the Labour Party in Britain showed the collapse of the workers' control theorists. Nationalised industries were to be run by semi-independent Public Corporations with freedom to regulate their day to day activities. There was provision for inclusion of some trade unionists as members of the Board of Public Corporations, but they were in no sense representatives of the trade unions. Immediately on their appointment, they had to sever their connections with the trade union of which they were members.

Growth of Nationalisation:

We shall now briefly trace the growth of nationalisation in East European countries, France and Britain.

East European Countries: The most spectacular and sweeping nationalisation programmes were executed in the East European countries after the defeat of the Axis powers. Even a casual glance at the extent of nationalisation will show the different significance of the measures in these countries and in, say, France and Britain. The nationalised industries of Poland and Czechoslovakia have become an integral part of the over-all planning of national economies. Despite a certain amount of resemblance between the British Public Corporations and the National Corporations responsible for running the nationalised industries in the two above-mentioned countries, the degree of influence exercised by the latter is considerably greater than the former[1]. By the Decree of October 24, 1945, in Czechoslovakia, 14 key industries, including all mines, power plants, iron and steel works, chemical and glass works, sugar factories and distilleries passed into state hands; private banks and insurance companies and, after the revolution, all establishments employing more than 50 workers were nationalised. Roughly speaking, 95% of the industry and all wholesale and foreign trade were under government control. In Poland, by 1938 the production of potassium salts, aircraft, automobiles and air transport, approximately 30% of production of tool-making machinery and some parts of natural gas, coal and chemicals had been nationalised[2]. On January 3, 1946, nationalisation measures were further extended affecting both the old and the new industries. Since 1949, about 90% of the manufacturing industries have passed into state control and ownership. In Rumania, too, under a Law of 1948, sweeping nationalisation measures were introduced, covering almost all industrial and commercial enterprises. Article 1 of this law brought under state ownership 77 different kinds of industrial undertakings. A Bulgarian Law of 1947 provided for the nationalisation of private industrial and mining enterprises. In some of these countries agriculture was the mainstay of the majority of

[1] Dorothy W. Douglas, *Transitional Economic Systems — The Polish-Czech Example*, Routledge and Kegan Paul Ltd., 1953: "The individual nationalised industries were in no sense sovereign states in the economy of the nation; at best they were provinces with some self-government. The difference between an economy with some elements of planning here and there and a "planned economy" is nowhere more evident than in this set of relationships". (p. 161).

[2] Samuel L. Sharp, *Nationalisation of Key Industries in Eastern Europe*, Foundation for Foreign Affairs, Washington, D.C. 1946.

people and nationalisation measures effected the expulsion of those people holding above a certain number of hectares of land. In Hungary, there are three laws dealing with the nationalisation of industrial enterprises in general, *viz.*, Law No. XXV of April 1948, Decree No. 20 of December 1950 and Decree No. 1 of January 1950. Besides this, there are three more laws dealing with special industries[1].

These sweeping nationalisation measures were occasioned by a large number of factors among which the widespread devastation caused by the war and the consequent difficulties in post-war adjustment were the most important. The entire economies of these countries had been so completely destroyed by the war that on its termination it had become essential to have some sort of economic planning which could re-shape the shattered economies on sounder lines. The increasing ideological impact of the Soviet Union, coupled with the local labour groups, some of whom had seized control of industries after the war, accelerated the tendency towards nationalisation as a step towards planning. In some countries where the economic machine had been subordinated to the German economic structure, the whole economy came down with the collapse of Germany. It was not possible to return the control to former owners, some of whom being Jews had fled the country, and some others who had collaborated with the Nazis. In the face of popular opposition, the private enterprisers, even if they had existed, would have been unable to shoulder the immense task of reconstruction. An extremely powerful resurgence of the spirit of nationalism that was strongly opposed to the re-entry of foreign capital, together with a passion for thorough-going economic planning in view of the tremendous war damage, had made nationalisation the inevitable course to adopt.

France: By 1935 there were 11 undertakings in France in which the State held either controlling interests or complete powers. After liberation from German occupation, France witnessed a popular demand for the nationalisation of some of its important industries. The opposition, too small in strength and consisting

[1] For some laws, see, *International and Comparative Law Quarterly*, January 1952, article by Joyce Gutteridge: "Expropriation and Nationalisation in Hungary, Bulgaria and Roumania", pp. 14–28.

of some conservative elements, was unable to stop the tide of popular insistence on this reform. It was expected that this measure would be meant not for improving some petty and transitory maladjustments, but for bringing about a basic change which would place in the hands of the government power over key industries so that it could also influence industries that were of lesser importance in the national economy. Accordingly, the Coal Mines (the coal mines of the Nord and Pas-de-Calais) were nationalised by an Order of December 13, 1944; all principal fuel undertakings, with the exception of national gas, mineral oils and peat, were taken over by the Act of May 17, 1946; the production, transport, distribution, import and export of Gas and Electricity passed into state hands by the Act of April 8, 1946 and insurance undertakings by the Act of April 25, 1946. The overwhelming enthusiasm seems to have waned now because of a number of difficulties, such as excessive delay in applying certain parts of the nationalisation laws and the failure of production to keep pace with the greatly increased demand.

Britain: In Britain before 1939, the Government had extended its control by setting up a number of Commissions and Corporations. The Forestry Commission of 1919, the Electricity Commission of 1920, the British Broadcasting Corporation of 1927, the London Passenger Transport Board of 1933, the British Overseas Airways Corporation of 1939 and some others had been established. There were great differences in the forms of organisation amongst these corporations, but they all were examples of increased governmental control and interference in different activities[1].

The Second World War had affected adversely the economy of Britain, and there was an urgent need for economic recovery. The Labour Party pledged itself to nationalise some of the important industries. Considering policy of full employment as essential for the revival of trade and industry, the party expressed its desire to achieve its goal by using to the maximum the productive capacity of the country; maintaining a high level of purchasing power through good wages, schemes of social services and taxation and a planned policy of investment, both

[1] For an enumeration and brief descriptions of the various bodies set up in Britain, see, D. N. Chester, *The Nationalised Industries — An Analysis of the Statutory Provisions*, Institute of Public Administration, London, 1951.

in the private and public sectors. Immediately on its return to power, the Labour Party set about executing its programme of nationalisation. In 1946, Acts were passed for the nationalisation of the Bank of England, of Cable and Wireless, Civil Aviation and the Coal Industry; in 1947, of Cotton (Centralized Buying), Electricity and Transport; in 1948, of Gas and in 1949, of Iron and Steel. Iron and Steel has since been denationalised.

Summary

The doctrine of *laissez-faire* was based on the following four assumptions; (i) the belief in the existence of a beneficent Natural Order, (ii) the idea of the inviolability of the right of an individual to private property, (iii) the assumption that every individual knew what was best for him and a supposed identity of interests between the individual and the society at large and, finally, (iv) the existence of perfect competition in the market. Its weakness lay in the fact that it ignored the implications of the unequal distribution of wealth. Moreover, the state of perfect competition had never existed. As trade and industry expanded, the numerous worker-employer conflicts, the increased maldistribution of wealth restricting effective demand in the market, the emergence of big combinations and existence of unemployment on a large-scale impelled the state to interfere in economic matters. Besides, the advent of war necessitated a central direction of the economy and the governments found themselves either actively directing the industries or taking over the ownership of those works which were essential for war purposes.

The advocates of nationalisation can be classified as (i) Non-socialists and (ii) Socialists, the former relying more on pragmatic grounds and the latter, generally speaking, regarding state ownership of industries as a necessary step for the change-over from capitalist to socialist society. Within the ranks of the Socialists, however, differences exist as to the methods of running the nationalised industries.

At the end of World War II, wholesale nationalisation of industries was carried out in the East European countries. In France and Britain, too, where the state had extended its control and ownership during the inter-war years, the proces of nationalisation was accelerated after the termination of the war.

CHAPTER II

SOME ASPECTS OF NATIONALISED COAL INDUSTRY

The Coal Industry Nationalisation Act[1] received the Royal Assent on July 12, 1946, and it was left to the Minister of Fuel and Power to decide on the date on which the industry was to be transferred to public ownership. The task was enormous and complex. A number of factors had to be taken into consideration before the final decision could be made. A change-over would have meant the cessation of activities by the numerous mining companies which were functioning in different parts of the country and a suitable organisation had to be evolved which could replace the existing one. Though activities in this direction had been started before the Vesting Day and the Board's members had been meeting frequently as an organising committee, the new organisation was far from complete. About 1500 collieries and ancillary undertakings employing a total number of about 800,000 persons were to be looked after. The Government's view was that any delay in the take-over of the industry would only result in prolonging the period of uncertainty. Accordingly the Minister of Fuel and Power informed the House of Commons that the Vesting Date would be 1st January 1947. On that date the industry passed into public ownership.

The Minister of Fuel & Power and the National Coal Board

Under the Coal Industry Nationalisation Act, a National Coal Board has been set up responsible to the Parliament and the public through the Minister of Fuel and Power. The Act has indicated the amount and nature of control which the Minister can exercise over the Board. The Board is granted a

[1] Coal Industry Nationalisation Act., 1946, 9 & 10 GEO. 6. CH. 59.

substantial degree of freedom to carry out its own activities. But the Minister may, after consultation with the Board, give to the latter "directions of a general character" on matters which appear to him as affecting the national interest. It was thought that any more detailed interference in the affairs of the Board by the Minister would tend to stifle the initiative without which the commercial success of the industry would be difficult to achieve. That would have defeated the purpose for which the operation of industry was placed in the hands of a Public Corporation[1]. Besides "directions of a general character", the Act mentions certain specific matters on which the Board has to consult the Minister. In framing programmes of reorganisation or development which require substantial outlay on capital account, the Board has to act on lines settled from time to time with the Minister's approval. Other topics on which the Board has to consult the Minister are problems of training, education and research. The Board keeps the Minister informed of its activities through an Annual Report. The Annual Reports are useful documents. They contain statistics pertaining to output of coal, tonnage lost through holidays, disputes, breakdowns, accidents, output per manshift, manpower, consumption, stocks and exports, average earnings of mineworkers etc. The financial directions issued by the Minister of Fuel and Power to the Board are also included therein.

The National Coal Board

Originally under the Act of 1946, the Board had one Chairman and eight other members who were appointed by the Minister of Fuel and Power. The Coal Industry Act, 1949, gave the Minister the power to increase the number of members to 12, of whom not more than eight, excluding the Chairman, should render whole-time service. Thereafter part-time members were appointed to the Board. The Act laid down that members should be chosen by the Minister "from amongst persons appearing to him to be qualified as having had experience of, and having shown capacity in, industrial, commercial or

---

[1] For characteristic features of Public Corporation, see: *Problems of Nationalized Industry*, W. A. Robson, (Ed.) Allen & Unwin Ltd., 1952, pp. 27–32.

financial matters, applied science, administration, or the organisation of workers"[1]. Originally, all members of the Board, except the Chairman and the Deputy Chairman, had departmental responsibilities. But the present Board is largely non-functional in character. Three members, however, are responsible for departments. These departments are: Labour Relations, Manpower and Welfare and Scientific. Besides these, the other departments at the London headquarters of the Board are: Finance, Marketing, Production, Carbonisation, Legal and Secretary's. The Secretary's Department looks after the general administrative work of the Board and concerns itself with the tasks which do not fall within the scope of any other department. The legal work of the Board is looked after by the Legal Department which is headed by a Legal Adviser. Both the Secretary and the Legal Adviser serve the Board as a whole and they report to the Chairman and the Deputy Chairman. The Board has also created certain Executive Committees, which are empowered to take decisions in the name of the Board. The proceedings of these committees are reviewed by the Board. Some of the important Committees are: General Purposes Committee, Personnel Committee, Organisation Committee, Finance Committee, Safety and Health Committee and Coke Committee.

The functions of the Board, as specified in the Act, can be summed up as follows; to work and get coal in Great Britain; to secure the efficient development of the coal-mining industry; to make supplies available of such qualities and in such quantities at prices which may further the public interest in all respects without showing any undue favour or advantage to anyone. In addition, the Board is also called upon to promote the safety, health and welfare of its employees and to secure the benefit of the practical experience of its employees in the operation of the industry. The Board has also to see that the industry pays its way over an average of good and bad years. In addition to the general enumeration of the duties in the Act, the Board in its capacity of the central organisation of the industry has to discharge a number of other functions. It has to formulate long-

[1] *op. cit.*, Sec. 2(3).

term economic plans for the industry and decide on a country-wide basis the direction and amount of capital investments needed in the industry. It has to watch and adjust the prices and discuss questions concerning wages, conditions of employment, etc., with the trade unions in the industry. As the apex of the organisational structure of the industry, the Board has to execute certain functions which cannot be delegated to any Divisional authority. Thus, the Board has to co-ordinate the selling arrangements of coal in such a way that the needs of the markets are properly balanced and matched with the differing sources of supply. Some other duties of the Board are: borrowing money from the Government to meet short and long-term requirements; arranging with the banks for the distribution of cash where it is wanted; taking care of legal proceedings in the High Court; answering queries from Members of Parliament and giving information to the public; dealing with Trade Associations whose commodities the Board needs for the industry, or selling to them its own products; taking care of the Training Centres which supply trained people to the industry; planning for miners' welfare; consulting other nationalised industries on matters of common interest; conducting scientific research and co-ordinating technical development[1].

Divisions

Unlike some other Nationalisation Acts, the Coal Industry Nationalisation Act, 1946, did not specify, apart from the setting-up of the N.C.B., the organisational structure which was to operate the industry and it was left to the N.C.B. to evolve its own set-up for running the industry. The Board created eight Divisions, each responsible for one of the main coalfields or group of coalfields in the country. These Divisions were: Scottish, Northern, North-Eastern, North-Western, East Midlands, West Midlands, South-Western and South-Eastern. A change in organisation was introduced towards the end of 1949, when the Northern Division was split up into two, *viz.*, Northern (Northumberland and Cumberland) and Durham. This separation was effected because the work of the

---

[1] N.C.B., *Report and Accounts for* 1948, pp. 113–114.

Northern Division was very heavy and it had to control about 200 collieries which were widely dispersed. The nine Divisions of the Coal Board are shown in the map below.

The Divisional Boards, which are collectively responsible to

the N.C.B., are modelled more or less on the same lines as the National Coal Board. They are composed of a Chairman, Deputy Chairman, (except in the case of the South-Eastern Division) and Directors who are in charge of Production, Marketing, Labour and Finance. While in the N.C.B., the departments of Labour Relations and Welfare are separate and are placed under two Board members, on the Divisional level both of them are merged into one. There is a Divisional Chief Scientist responsible to the Divisional Board as a whole. The members of the Divisional Board are selected for their experience in the coal industry. Originally, all the Chairmen were appointed from outside the industry and were men with considerable knowledge of administration and affairs. The pattern has now undergone some changes.

The Divisions are an intermediate authority between the N.C.B. and the Areas. The Divisions explain the N.C.B.'s view-point to the Areas and also try to acquaint the national head-quarters with regional and local conditions. The N.C.B. decided that to make the Areas directly responsible to itself would result in over-centralisation. The absence of Divisions, it was thought, would mean constant references to London and administrative delays would deny to the industry the flexibility which was necessary for its commercial success.

A number of regional functions are discharged by the Divisions. These could neither be taken up by the N.C.B. nor could they be left to the Areas. The Divisions are about the right size as units for the co-ordination of regional selling. It is the duty of the Divisions to appoint or recommend the appointment of Area General Managers and to hold them to account for their activities. The Divisions employ production experts whose technical knowledge and experience is available to all the areas functioning within a particular Division. The Techincal Advisory Committee, — known as the "Reid" Committee — had drawn attention to the shortage of mining engineers in the country and had suggested that the services of the engineers should be used for the wider benefits of the industry. In this sense, the Divisions provide regional pools of technical expertise from where such knowledge is disseminated to the Areas. Other common services provided by the Divisional organisations include advice on legal questions, audit services, etc. Widespread strikes, which extend beyond the boundaries of a single Area, are also handled by the Boards. The Boards also discuss with trade unions regional wage settlements.

The Divisional Boards command a wide measure of delegated authority. They were set up by the N.C.B. to bring about as much devolution of authority as possible. The Divisional Boards are authorized to sanction, without reference to the N.C.B., schemes of reconstruction which do not involve a capital expenditure of more than £ 250,000. These schemes have to conform to the pattern of reorganisation as enunciated in the "National Plan". It has been estimated that of the first £ 100 million invested in the industry after nationalisation more than 75% of the expenditure was sanctioned by Divisional Boards without reference to the N.C.B.[1].

Areas

The nine Divisions are further divided into 50 (the number has been changing from time to time) Areas, and each Division controls a certain number of Areas. In deciding upon the size of the Areas, the N.C.B. kept in mind the recommendations of the "Reid Report". The Report had commented adversely on the uneconomic size of many colliery companies which, because of their smallness, could in many cases not even maintain essential staff and services. The N.C.B., therefore, had to strike upon the optimum size which could be large enough for providing essential services such as laboratories, workshops, planning staffs, etc., and yet not be too large for administrative purposes. Factors of geography, geology and physical distances had to be taken into consideration. Naturally, therefore, the sizes of Areas vary considerably. Some large areas are divided into sub-Areas for purposes of administrative convenience. The average Area has an output of about 4 million tons, a yearly turnover of about £ 10 million and employs about 16,000 men. Thus an Area is a very large commercial undertaking and the success or failure of the industry depends to a great extent on the efficiency with which the Areas are organised and operated.

The Area organisation is headed by an Area General Manager who is answerable to the Divisional Board for everything that happens within his Area. He is assisted by a team of experts on production and labour problems, marketing, finance and science who advise him in their special fields. But there is nothing like a set pattern of organisation and variations have been introduced

[1] N.C.B., *Some Notes on the British Coal Industry*, p. 3.

in response to local needs. Through its various Departments, the Area organisation handles the correspondence with all the collieries under its charge and with the Division, prepares plans for the long-term development of collieries, deals with labour disputes, conducts scientific experiments like testing of dusts in the mines, handles the purchase of stores for the collieries, to a certain extent markets coal produced in the Area, keeps accounts and reviews capital expenditures incurred in the Area.

Collieries

The collieries are the last units in the organisation of the coal-mining industry. But they are the most important since coal is produced there. It is in the collieries that the overwhelming manpower of the industry is employed. The great differences in the size and geological conditions of the pits make for variations in the organisation of the mines. These differences, along with the traditions of each pit which have become rigid with the passage of time, give to each mine a uniqueness which defies the application of standardized measures. However, broadly speaking the organisation of the mines is more or less similar, and, without going into the technical details, we will now briefly describe the organisation of pits.

Each pit is headed by a Manager who has an over-all responsibility for the working and safety of the men in the pit. The main legislative provisions as contained in the Coal Mines Act of 1911 lay down the duties and qualifications of a Manager. At some of the very large pits, the Manager is assisted by an Assistant Manager. At most sizeable collieries there are one or more Undermanagers. The Undermanager is in charge of all underground operations during his tour of duty. The duties of the Undermanager generally are: ordering from the colliery stores the materials needed for the day-to-day use in the pit; placing men on special tasks, like opening up new "districts"[1]; distribution of week-end work; checking allowances to be paid to the workers; and, in some coalfields, engaging or dismissing

---

[1] A "District" is "an area of the mine containing, usually, a working face and forming a district section of the ventilation system, with its own "intake" and "returns" roads".
Coal Mining, Published by the N.C.B., p. 14.

workers. Next in line of command is the Overman who takes charge of a whole shift underground in one section of the workings. His main function is to see that his men, who might

ORGANISATION OF THE COAL INDUSTRY

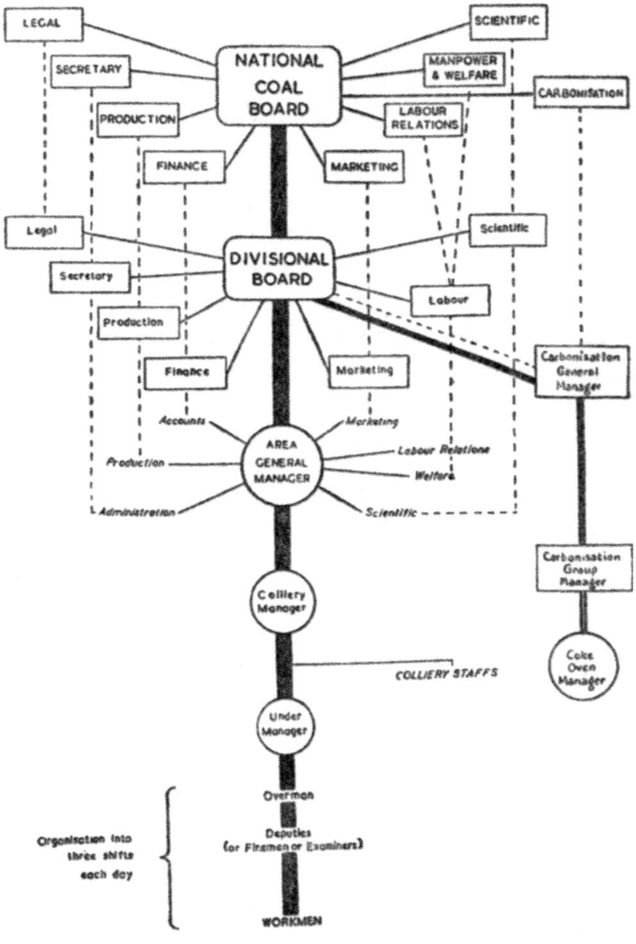

Source: *Coal Mining*, Published by N.C.B.

be working in different places below ground, are doing work which will carry forward the Manager's plan for the development of the pit. Then follow the Deputies (or Firemen or Examiners) who are responsible for "districts". Lastly, under the Deputies are groups of workmen, generally headed by chargemen, who are responsible for cutting the coal and transporting it to the surface. At most of the collieries work goes on for all the twenty-four hours and is divided among three main "shifts" of 7½ hours each, plus one winding-time. [1] Though workers in different shifts do somewhat different work, their work as a whole fits together and forms a certain "cycle of operations" every twenty-four hours. In addition to the above, the collieries employ other administrative and technical staff like Engineers, Surveyors, Training Officers, Safety Officers and Storekeepers.

Trade Unions in Coal-Mining

The Nationalisation Act of 1946 makes it obligatory on the Board to enter into consultation with organisations which appear to it to be representative of substantial proportions of the persons employed in the industry. On taking over the industry the Board had to ascertain the representative character of the different organisations so that it could establish joint conciliation and consultative machinery with them. As a result discussions were held with the following organisations:

The National Union of Mineworkers: An overwhelming majority of the employees of the industry are organized in the N.U.M., and for this reason the N.U.M. plays a very important part in the negotiations and consultations which take place between the workers and the Board. Though the importance of N.U.M. in the industry cannot be over-emphasized, the fact must not be forgotten that the key position of some other employees' organisations makes them important despite their numerical insignificance. We shall consider this point in Chapter V when we discuss the Officials' Disputes which took place in the year 1952.

The N.U.M. assumed its present centralized form in 1945. It was in that year that the loosely-linked District Unions were unified into a strong central organisation. All grades of labour employed in mining are organized and represented by the N.U.M

The British Association of Colliery Management: The B.A.C.M. represents the majority of managerial, professional and technical

[1] "Winding Time" means the time taken to get a whole shift from the surface to the place of work underground. It takes, generally speaking, about 30 minutes.

grades. Previously the National Association of Colliery Managers was the only body which represented the colliery managers. But it was essentially a professional organisation and was precluded by its charter from negotiating on the terms and conditions of employment of its members. The B.A.C.M. was registered as a trade union and the Board accepted it as the representative organisation of many of the managerial grades from Undermanager upwards. Conciliation machinery was set up between the Board and the B.A.C.M. by an agreement signed on June 6, 1948. In 1949 the Board also recognised the Association as the body to negotiate on behalf of other grades of staff, whose status was comparable or superior to Undermanagers. In case of some borderline staff, the B.A.C.M. was accepted as one of the bodies representing the interests of "scientific technologists" and engineering draughtsmen. In 1949 the Board also recognized the B.A.C.M. as representative of some grades of labour officers, but later on this recognition was withdrawn.

The National Association of Colliery Overmen, Deputies and Shotfirers: The N.A.C.O.D.S. was recognized as a body representative of the Deputies employed in the industry. The Association also claimed that it should be allowed to represent Overmen and Shotfirers. But the Board found that the N.U.M. also had Overmen and Shotfirers among its members. Both the N.A.C.O.D.S. and the N.U.M. were recognized jointly as representing the Overmen and Shotfirers[1].

The National Union of Colliery Winding Enginemen: The National Union of Colliery Winding Enginemen was formed in January 1947 and was composed of several district unions some of which had broken away from the N.U.M. This Union was not recognized by the Board. The Winding Enginemen who were members of the N.U.M. were covered by conciliation arrangements made between the N.U.M. and the N.C.B. A dispute ensued and the National Union of Colliery Winding Enginemen claimed recognition. The matter was referred to a Court of Inquiry who, while sympathising with the underlying motives of the Winding

[1] Also see Chapter V, the Officials' Disputes (1952).

Enginemen, did not agree that "it would be in the interests of the industry as a whole, or indeed of Winding Enginemen as one section of a class in the industry, that an organisation representing a section of them should be recognized by the National Coal Board as a separate entity outside the existing conciliation machinery for the purpose of negotiating conditions of employment"[1]. The Court, however, suggested that effective steps should be taken inside the N.U.M. to give adequate representation to Winding Enginemen when questions concerning the latter are discussed. Another breakaway Union called the Colliery Winders' Federation of Great Britain was formed in September 1948 following the 18th Award of the National Reference Tribunal. Subsequently in 1951 this organisation was absorbed in the N.U.M. and the separate existence of the Colliery Winders' Federation ceased.

Organisations representing workers at Coke Oven and By-Product Plants: There were three organisations which represented the workers at Coke oven and By-Product Plants. These were: the National Union of Blast-furnacemen, Ore Miners, Coke Workers, and Kindred Trades, the National Union of General and Municipal Workers and the N.U.M. The first named organisation withdrew and by an arrangement made between the remaining two unions, the N.U.M. was empowered to negotiate on behalf of both. In 1948 the Board and the N.U.M. drew up conciliation machinery for workers at Coke-Ovens and By-Product plants.

Clerical Staff: In 1946 the Board asked the Trade Union Congress to suggest as to which organisations should be considered representative of the clerical staff employed by the Board at its Area, Divisional and National Headquarters. The Congress advised that the Clerical and Administrative Workers' Union would be the suitable body for Headquarters and the National Association of Clerical and Supervisory Staffs for Divisions. For the staff at the Area levels and below, the Board was able to draw up an agreement in 1951 with the C.A.W.U., N.U.M., and N.A.C.S.S. Thus all the three organisations appear in the

[1] *Report of a Court of Inquiry into a dispute between the National Coal Board and the National Union of Colliery Winding Enginemen*, H.M.S.O., 1948, p. 13.

picture when negotiations take place concerning the clerical staff at Area levels.

Machinery for Conciliation

As already mentioned, the N.C.B. has the statutory obligation of concluding agreements with representative workers' and employees' organisations for the establishment and maintenance of joint machinery for

(a) the settlement by negotiation of terms and conditions of employment, with provision for reference to arbitration in default of such settlement in such cases as may be determined by or under the agreements; and

(b) consultation on —

(i) questions relating to the safety, health or welfare of such persons;

(ii) the organisation and conduct of the operations in which such persons are employed and other matters of mutual interest to the Board and such persons arising out of the exercise and performance by the Board of their functions[1].

The above two clauses also indicate the difference between conciliation and consultation in the coal industry. The conciliation machinery in the industry is required to deal with matters concerning wages and conditions of employment. The consultative machinery, on the other hand, handles matters pertaining to the safety, health and welfare of the employees in the coal industry. In practice, however, certain subjects might overlap, or a subject falling within the jurisdiction of the conciliation machinery may raise problems which can be discussed in consultative bodies[2].

We will take up conciliation first. Before nationalisation, a National Conciliation Scheme was in existence in the industry. The scheme was established as the result of the efforts of the Greene Board[3], which was charged, *inter alia*, with the task

---

[1] Coal Industry Nationalisation Act, 1946, Sec. 46(1) (a) and (b).

[2] On this point, see, *The Framework of Joint Consultation*, The Acton Society Trust, 1952, pp. 2–3.

[3] *Third Report of the Board of Investigation Into Wages and Machinery for determining Wages and Conditions of Employment in the Coal-Mining Industry*, H.M.S.O., 1943.

For earlier period, see, Ian G. Sharp, *Industrial Conciliation and Arbitration*, Allen & Unwin Ltd., 1950, Part I, Chap. II.

"to enquire into the present machinery and methods of determining wages and conditions of employment in the industry, and to submit recommendations for the establishment of a procedure and permanent machinery for dealing with questions of wages and conditions of employment in the industry". The Committee recommended the establishment of a National Conciliation Board consisting of (i) a Joint National Negotiating Committee and (ii) a National Reference Tribunal. The important features of the National Conciliation Scheme were as follows: (i) It provided a comprehensive method of settling all questions of a national character; (ii) District autonomy, a fundamental element in the structure of the industry, was left untouched by handing over the settlement of purely district questions to the district conciliation machinery; (iii) Any district question of special importance could be transferred to the National machinery; and (iv) It provided for the immediate establishment of proper conciliation machinery for the final settlement of purely district questions, and where not already in existence, such machinery was to be set up by special district agreements conforming to certain minimum requirements considered necessary by the Committee for efficient working[1].

When the industry was nationalised, the existing conciliation machinery was taken over with slight modifications. The machinery has a three-tier structure, *viz.*, the National, the District and the Pit. At all the three levels, provision is made for settling disputes through negotiation, and negotiation failing, there is provision for referring disputes to arbitration the awards of which are binding on both sides. In addition to the conciliation machinery between the N.C.B. and the N.U.M., there are separate arrangements concerning the managerial and other grades of employees in the service of the N.C.B.[2] However, the N.U.M.

---

[1] *Third Report of the Board of Investigation, op. cit.*, p. 2.

[2] For Conciliation Agreements with workers in Coke and By-Product Industry and with the British Association of Colliery Management, see *Memorandum of Agreements, Arbitration Awards and Decisions, Recommendations and Interpretations Relating to National Questions Concerning Wages and Conditions of Employment in the Coalmining Industry of Great Britain*, National Coal Board, Part III, 1st January to 31st December, 1948, pp. 274–303 and 360–378 respectively.

The N.C.B. has done a useful service by bringing together in bound. volumes copies of all Agreements, Arbitration awards, etc., from 1940 onwards.

being the most important and massive of all workers' organisations in the industry, we shall restrict ourselves to outlining the conciliation scheme between the N.C.B. and the N.U.M.

Each side, the N.C.B. and the N.U.M., is represented by sixteen members on the Joint National Negotiating Committee who meet together to discuss and reach agreement on national questions in the industry. There are two Chairmen, one on each side, and two Joint Secretaries. Voting is by sides. There is a time limit of generally five weeks within which agreement has to be reached. Failing this, the matter is referred to the National Reference Tribunal (generally known as the "Porter" Tribunal, after its Chairman, Lord Porter). The Tribunal consists of three members who are in no way connected with the coal industry. They are appointed by the Master of Rolls after consultation with the Board and the Union. Their term of appointment is five years. When a question is referred to the National Reference Tribunal, the Negotiating Committee chooses four assessors, two from each side, to help the Tribunal in obtaining all the facts. These assessors, however, have nothing to do with the final verdict of the Tribunal.

For settling district questions, the whole industry has been divided into 18 wage districts. In each of these districts, a District Conciliation Board has been established. The Divisional Coal Board and the Area organisation of the N.U.M. are represented on these Boards. A difficulty was experienced since the N.U.M. Areas were not co-extensive with the Coal Board's Divisions. Despite some reorganisation in the Union's Areas, the District Conciliation Boards sometimes find themselves discussing the issue with more than one Area Unions of the N.U.M. The District Conciliation Boards function in much the same way as the Joint National Negotiating Committee. If any question is not settled by the Board within the specified time-limit, which is generally three weeks, the matter is then referred to the arbitration of a District Referee whose appointment has been accepted by the two sides of the District Conciliation Board. There is provision for referring a matter, which is being discussed as a District question, to the Joint National Negotiating Committee, if it is considered that the question under discussion has a wider significance than that of the District.

When the Conciliation Scheme was adapted to the needs of the nationalised coal industry, both the N.C.B. and the N.U.M. recognized the importance of providing machinery which could settle speedily and effectively the day-to-day disputes which were bound to arise at the pits. The scheme which has been adopted in the coalfields has the same basic principles as the National and District schemes, *viz.*, negotiation and, failing negotiation, arbitration. There is also provision for a Pit question to be transferred to higher levels if the issue is of wider significance. The scheme at the pits is operated by means of the following six stages:

(1) When a dispute arises at a pit, the issue is discussed between the workmen concerned and the immediate pit official.

(2) If the dispute is not settled within three days at the first stage, it is then discussed between the colliery Manager and the workmen concerned.

(3) At the third stage the Trade Union official takes over from the workmen. If the dispute is not settled here within three days, it then enters the fourth stage.

(4) The dispute is then formally presented before a Pit meeting, consisting of representatives of the Management and the Union. The meeting is to be held within five days of the request for such a meeting. It has to accomplish its work within two weeks.

(5) Failing settlement at the fourth stage, the matter is referred to the appropriate Disputes Committee. These committees are set up by the mutual agreement of the two sides of the District Conciliation Board. The Disputes Committees are given two weeks at their disposal for settling the issue.

(6) The failure of the Disputes Committee to settle the matter takes the issue to the sixth and the final stage of the Pit Conciliation machinery. The unsettled question is referred for arbitration to the District Umpire whose verdict on a Pit question is both final and binding.

Machinery for Joint Consultation

Joint consultation between the employers and the workers is not new in coal-mining, nor was it introduced when the industry was nationalised. Attempts had been made to evolve methods for joint consultation in the industry during World War I. The

Mining Industry Act of 1920 had also contributed in this direction. During the second World War a more serious effort was made by establishing what were called the Pit Production Committees[1]. Though it has been said that on the whole the Pit Production Committees failed to achieve their purpose, viz., stepping up production, "they did useful work in the sphere of industrial relations and they provided a potential implement of co-operation between the managing elements in the pits and the mineworkers"[2].

The Consultative machinery in the industry at present is as follows:

On the national level, there is a National Consultative Council which has within its purview all the undertakings in the industry. Its functions, as specified in its constitution, are to consult with representative organisations on matters which fall within the term "consultation" to the exclusion of subjects connected with wages and conditions of employment. The Council consists of twenty-seven members, of whom six are appointed by the N.C.B., nine by the N.U.M., nine by the National Association of Colliery Managers and three by the National Association of Colliery Overmen, Deputies and Shotfirers. The Council is presided over by the Chairman of the N.C.B. and the other organisations on the Council elect a Deputy Chairman each. The Council meets once a month, though the consideration of an urgent matter might increase the frequency of the meetings. The Council has the right to appoint Committees for examining special issues for which purpose the Council may authorise the committees to co-opt persons with special knowledge of the matter under discusison. The organisations represented on the Council are free to submit any items for inclusion in the agenda of the meetings. Attempt is made by the Council to reach agreement by mutual consent and persuasion, but the differing opinions are placed on record so that the Coal Board may derive the greatest advantage from the proceedings of the Council.

[1] A very interesting account of the Pit Production Committees will be found in: W. H. B. Court, *Coal*, History of the Second World War, United Kingdom Civil Series, Edited by W. K. Hancock, H.M.S.O., and Longmans, Green and Co., 1951, pp. 317–323.

[2] *ibid.*, p. 322.

The Divisional and Area Consultative Councils are modelled on the same lines as the National Consultative Council. They cover their own Divisions and Areas. The Divisional Councils consist of 19 members, excluding the Chairman, who is the Chairman of the Divisional Board. Out of 19 members, five are appointed by the Board, six by the N.U.M., six by the N.A.C.M., and two by the N.A.C.O.D.S. The Area Consultative Councils consist of a Chairman and twelve other members of whom five are appointed by the Area General Manager, five by the N.U.M., one by the N.A.C.M., and one by the N.A.C.O.D.S. The Area General Manager acts as the Chairman of the Area Consultative Council.

The most important unit in the whole machinery of consultation is the Colliery Consultative Committee. The preamble to the Constitution of the Colliery Consultative Committees reads as follows: "In a publicly owned Coalmining Industry the concern of managements and workmen should be identical. It is expedient, therefore, to set up a consultative body at each colliery with the object of securing the closest co-operation amongst all those concerned in the operation of the colliery". The terms of reference of the Colliery Consultative Committees are the same as those of Area, Divisional and National Consultative Councils with difference in their jurisdictions. Besides the general functions of consulting with, and advising, the colliery management on matters of health, welfare and safety of workers, the following subjects are considered by the Colliery Consultative Committees.

(1) The accidents and sickness trends for the colliery and measures for reducing them;

(2) looking after the colliery welfare arrangements, such as the proper provision of meals, washing accommodation, sanitation, first-aid equipment, schemes to provide a common service for laundering, etc.;

(3) the training and educational activities associated with the collieries;

(4) the technical efficiency of the colliery, for which purpose figures of output are examined and measures are designed to increase productivity;

(5) to find out ways and means whereby the active support

of the workmen and the local lodge can be enlisted for the activities of the Committee;

(6) formulation of current and future development plans for the colliery;

(7) any other relevant matter referred to the Committee by the Area Consultative Council[1].

The colliery Manager acts as the Chairman of the Committee and is assisted by a Vice-Chairman who is chosen from amongst the members. The Area Agent and the Lodge Secretary of the N.U.M. and the Mining Agent act as ex-officio members. Out of the three members appointed by the Manager, two are underground officials and one is a surface official. A Deputy is elected by secret ballot of the Deputies. Six other members are elected by secret ballot from nominations submitted by the N.U.M. Branch. These six members represent the five main grades of workers, *viz.*, face worker, underground haulage worker, contract worker not employed at the face, surface worker (including checkweighmen), and tradesman. Two of the six members are face workers. The candidates for election have to satisfy three conditions: (i) they should be employed at the colliery for not less than 12 consecutive months before the date of election; (ii) they should be members of a Trade Union which is representative of their grade in the industry; and (iii) they should be engaged in the grade for which they are nominated. The size of the Committee can be smaller than the usual one if the Divisional Consultative Council thinks that the size of the colliery warrants such a measure.

The Colliery Consultative Committees meet fortnightly, but where advisable, the frequency of meetings can be increased. A Secretary is responsible for keeping the minutes and for discharging other secretarial duties concerning the activities of the Committee. The Colliery officers such as those who are in charge of training, safety, health and welfare attend the meetings when their presence is deemed essential by the Committee. When a matter is not settled in the Committee and difference of opinion exists, it can be, if the members so wish, referred to the Area Labour Officer whose duty it is then to try to reconcile the differences.

[1] *Guide to Consultation*, Published by the N.C.B., p. 33.

Miners' Welfare[1]

Organised welfare schemes in the mining industry go back to the year 1920 when the Mining Industry Act established the Miners' Welfare Fund. The Fund was fed by a levy on coal output and the amount was charged, with the exception of seven years in the 1930's, at the rate of 1d. a ton on saleable output. The fund thus created was used for the social well-being of workers in or about coal mines and for mining research and education. A second levy of 1s. in the pound on mining royalties was introduced by the Mining Industry Act, 1926. This was to provide funds for the construction of pithead baths. The Miners' Welfare Commission was reponsible for administering these funds.

The Coal Industry Nationalisation Act, 1946, confirmed the existence of the Miners' Welfare Commission, and also laid a statutory obligation on the N.C.B. to arrange for the welfare of its employees. The output levy under the old arrangement was to cease at the end of 1951, and in order to plan for future welfare arrangements, the N.C.B. and the N.U.M. opened discussions in 1950. The result was the drawing up of an Agreement signed on July 24, 1951[2]. The necessary statutory effect to its provisions was given by the passage of the Miners' Welfare Act, 1952. Welfare in the industry is now divided into two categories: "Colliery Welfare" and "Social Welfare".

"Colliery Welfare", which is the Board's responsibility, includes "all activities which are conducive to the well-being of persons employed in and connected with the Coal Industry, considered as workers and as members of the organisations in which they work..."[3] The main activities undertaken in this direction are: provision of pithead baths, canteens, medical services, vocational education and training for employment in the coal industry, suitable and convenient accommodation for workers in the industry, attention to the individual needs of the workers affecting their work, excluding those covered by wages

---

[1] Our description is based largely on the *1st Annual Report of the Coal Industry Social Welfare Organisation*, 1952, issued from their registered office, 5, Hobart Place, London.

[2] For the text of the Agreement, see, N.C.B., *Memorandum of Agreements, etc.*, Part VI, 1st January to 31st December, 1951, pp. 162–170.

[3] *ibid.*, clause 2.

and conditions of service, welfare of the sick and of those disabled by accidents and their resettlement at work on their return.

"Social Welfare", which is the responsibility of a newly created body called the Coal Industry Social Welfare Organisation, includes "all activities which are conducive to the well-being of persons employed in or connected with the Coal Industry and all other persons employed by the Board, and of their families, considered as citizens and as members of the community..."[1] The main activities organised by the C.I.S.W.O. are: the encouragement of sports and games, social and cultural activities, provision of youth clubs and camps, organizing holiday camps and the encouragement of education in all fields other than vocational training for the industry. The activities of the C.I.S.W.O. are financed by grants made from time to time by the N.C.B. This was specified in Section 13 of the Miners' Welfare Act, 1952. The Articles of Association of the Organisation provide that the Council of the Organisation, which is the main executive body, shall be composed of up to six Directors appointed by the N.C.B., at least one of whom shall be from the managerial grade and up to six Directors appointed by the N.U.M., one of whom shall be appointed by the N.A.C.O.D.S. On 1st July 1952 a Coal Industry Social Welfare Scheme was drawn up. The main working principles of the scheme can be summed up as follows. First, the Council of Organisation has been keen to avoid centralisation and to devolve as much responsibility as is consistent with maintaining its own authority. Experience had shown that the operation of the Miners' Welfare Commission was centralized. This had given rise to delays in the sanction and execution of new projects. In the present set-up, therefore, nine Divisional Welfare Committees have been established which are responsible for approving the details of social welfare projects within their jurisdiction. These schemes have, however, to conform to the general lines indicated by the Council of the Organisation. Secondly, attempts are made to co-ordinate, so far as is possible, the activities of the Organisation with the Colliery Welfare work of the Board. The desirability of this measure is particularly apt in the case of miners' welfare,

---

[1] *ibid.*, clause 3.

because welfare provisions at the colliery such as pit-head baths and canteens are as important to the miner as to his family. The co-ordination is sought to be achieved by the stipulation that the Joint Honorary Secretaries of each Welfare Committee shall be one from the Board and one from the Union. Thirdly, co-operation is also sought with public authorities and other organisations interested in social welfare services. Fourthly, the Organisation attempts to break down the segregation of the mining communities from the rest of the society. Fifthly, the principle of parity of representation between the Board and the Union is observed throughout the entire structure of the Council of Organisation and other bodies set up for purposes of promoting miners' welfare.

Manpower

When the industry passed into national ownership, the Coal Board was faced with a serious shortage of manpower and since then the Board has been busy devising ways and means whereby a larger manpower can be recruited and maintained in the industry.

The War-period: The figure for manpower had been steadily declining since 1920. In that year the total labour force in the industry was 1,200,000, but by 1940 it had gone down to less than 750,000. The situation became serious during the early phases of the war and it can be said that since then it has never been satisfactory. When the war broke out, the industry employed about 765,000 wage-earners, and about 53,000 additional miners were registered as unemployed. The collapse of France resulted in the loss of export markets for British coal and severe unemployment set in in certain mining areas. But by 1941 when the economic machinery had been increasingly mobilised for war purposes, the internal demand for coal registered a sharp rise. The Government failed to foresee the increase in demand in the near future, and when coal-mining was called upon to produce more, the industry found itself hopelessly under-manned. Thousands of miners had left the coalfields and joined the armed forces or found new work in the industries which had sprung up in response to war-time demands. In June 1941 an appeal made by the Minister of Labour to the ex-miners to return voluntarily to the pits did not meet with much success. In July, therefore, a scheme for compulsory registration of all ex-miners between the ages of 20–60, who had been employed in the mines from 1935 onwards, was introduced. The figure of ex-miners thus registered came to over 105,000 but out of this less than 26,000 stated that they were prepared to return to mining. The number of miners who actually returned to mining was still smaller. The slow progress of the re-employment of the unemployed miners and the "imperfect co-ordination of the transfer of an ex-miner back to the industry with his acceptance for work by an employer" were the two factors responsible for this[1]. But besides these, the low level of wages and the unpleasant nature of the task in mining made the miner reluctant to go back to the pit. The Forster Committee, which submitted its report in July 1942, summed up the causes of low recruitment as follows: (i) widespread unemployment in the industry after World War I and the resulting sense of economic insecurity among the miners; (ii) the low rates of wages as compared to other industries; (iii) the difficult and dangerous nature of the work underground; (iv) the reluctance of the miner parents to allow their sons to enter mining; (v) the increased possibilities of employment for work outside the mining valleys; and (vi) a decline in the birth-rate in the mining families after the General Strike of 1926. According to one source, the net intake or outflow in the industry was as follows: in 1942, a net gain of 7,679; in 1943, a net loss of 8,843; in 1944, a net gain of 12,046; in 1945, a net loss of 17,351[2].

1947 *and after and the Coal Board's efforts:* Thus when the National Coal Board took over the industry, it was faced with a serious shortage of manpower and since then it has been struggling against this problem. The following figures of net intake and outflow, taken from the Coal Board's Annual Reports, show the position of manpower from the year 1946 to 1953.

---

[1] International Labour Office, *Wartime Transference of Labour in Great Britain*, Montreal, 1943, p. 41.

[2] Cmd. 6920, Table 13, quoted in W.H.B. Court, *op. cit.*, p. 297.

	Years			
Net intake	1946	1947	1948	1949
or outflow	— 4,198	+ 26,165	+ 7,751	— 16,397

	Years			
Net intake	1950	1951	1952	1953
or outflow	— 20,522	+ 9,307	+ 22,594	— 10,891

(The figure for 1947 is for 53 weeks, the others for 52 weeks).

During 1947 the manpower target set by the Government for the Board was to get 730,000 men on colliery books by the end of the year. After providing for wastage, it meant recruiting a number of 100,000 persons. This was not an easy task. Recruitment in mining does not only mean finding people and putting them to work in the pits. The new-comers have to undergo training and training facilities at the disposal of the Board were then limited. Shortage of housing was another difficulty. From April 1, the Board took over recruitment in its own hands and a campaign was started to get as many men in the industry as possible. Coal was an important element in putting Britain on the road to economic recovery. Internal demand, therefore, was high. Besides, the war had left many European countries economically prostate and coal was needed for their recovery too. Efforts were made by the Board to enlist persons who could be put on the face-work or whose recruitment could release the oncost workers to be upgraded to work on the faces. Early in the year a number of Poles were also recruited from the Polish Resettlment Corps. Despite the willingness of the National Union of Mineworkers, a number of lodges opposed the recruitment of Polish, and later of Italian, workers. Arrangements for training facilities for the new recruits were expanded and the Government was approached to ease the housing shortage for miners. Existing hostel facilities were extended. Despite all these efforts, the year ended with a total manpower of 718,000, that is, about 12,000 short of the target. The quick changes in organisation at collieries during the year 1948 made it difficult to forecast accurately the manpower which was needed. The Board's target was 750,000, but the actual figure at the end of the year was only 726,300. Housing shortage continued to be an obstructing factor and the raising of the school-leaving age also reduced the number of juvenile recruits available for the industry. The number of miners who were released from the

Forces and who returned to take up employment in the mines also declined. During 1949 the Board's efforts were directed at increasing the manpower at coalface by upgrading other workers employed underground. Increased mechanization and more efficient methods of transport systems were adopted which released more men who were to be employed at coal-cutting jobs at the faces. It was estimated that about 10,000 men would be needed to replace the men who were to be upgraded. However, the fall in the number of ex-miners returning from the Forces, the rise in the school-leaving age and the reduced number of British adult recruits resulted in a manpower decline of over 16,000 men. The more effective employment of the existing labour force, however, saved the industry from the serious loss in production which would otherwise have occurred due to the loss in manpower. In some Divisions, Scotland for example, the problem was to transfer the men from the less to the more productive fields. Despite the shortage of manpower, the Board did not want to keep in service the inefficient hands, and it requested the Government to remove the "Ring Fence"[1]. The recruitment of juveniles, though higher in 1949 as compared to 1948, was not enough. The year 1950 witnessed an acute manpower shortage in many coalfields and there was a net outflow from the industry of 20,522 men. In some areas the shortage of men employed in underground jobs became so acute that a number of face-workers had to be withdrawn to fill up the gaps. Efforts to recruit juveniles resulted in about 15,000 joining the industry during 1950. A fresh publicity campaign on a large-scale was started in 1951 by the Board in collaboration with the Ministry of Labour and National Service to get more men in the industry. A scheme devised in the early part of 1951 to recruit Italians met with stiff opposition from some lodges of the Union. As a result of these efforts, the net manpower gain in the industry in 1951 was 9,307. The number of juveniles who joined the industry in 1951 was 20,000 as compared to 15,000 in 1950 and 14,000 in 1949. The year 1952 recorded a net intake of 22,594 men in the industry. The figure of wastage declined

[1] The term "Ring Fence" implied that when a worker had been in the industry for three months, he could not leave without the permission of the Minister of Labour, though he was free to move from one colliery to another.

and the number of juvenile recruits went up. It had been estimated that about 713,000 men would be required in the industry by the end of 1952, but this figure had been surpassed by the middle of April 1952. The target was further raised to 724,000 men and efforts were made not only to recruit more men, but also to recruit them at the right places. In order to achieve the latter aim, the Board introduced a scheme of transfer allowances for miners who were to move from one part of the country to another. To counteract the shortage of housing, the Coal Industry Housing Association was formed to carry out a special programme for building houses in areas where the local authorities could not build houses quickly enough for the needs of the mining population. The number of juveniles recruited in 1952 went up to 27,000. An increase in the number of face-workers was also recorded. At the beginning of 1953 the total labour force in the industry was 720,700. During the year there was a net outflow of about 11,000 men from the industry. The number of face-workers, however, remained steady at about 300,000. Nearly 6,000 houses were completed and were occupied by the miners. The recruitment of juveniles during the year was fairly good.

We have traced briefly the manpower situation in the industry over the country as a whole. Needless to say, this over-all picture does not bring out the varying degrees of intensity with which manpower shortage is experienced in different Divisions and Areas of the Coal Board.

It must be recognized that the task of the Coal Board in trying to recruit adequate manpower for the industry is a formidable one. In a full-employment economy, coal-mining will, by the very nature of its task, find it difficult to attract enough recruits. Unless the difficult and dangerous nature of the task is amply compensated by adequate wages, good and safe working conditions and comfortable living facilities, mining would continue to show an insufficient manpower. In this sense the efforts of the Board towards expanding welfare facilities, mitigating the scourge of pneumoconiosis, reducing absenteeism, improving safety methods in order to reduce the number of accidents, making wage-scales attractive, providing housing accommodation and improving industrial relations will all contribute towards solving the problem of manpower. Clearly a detailed discussion of all these topics is outside our scope. We may say that the Board has been making efforts in three directions to solve the problem of manpower shortage: (i) trying to make a more effective use of the existing manpower; (ii) getting more men into the industry by publicizing the benefits which the miners are entitled to; and (iii) transferring men to the places where they are needed most. The Board is devoting special attention to the recruitment of juveniles in the interests of long-term considerations of the industry. A "Ladder Plan" was worked out in 1949 by the Board which will "give every young recruit to mining a chance of systematic training for a career and improve the standard of technical knowledge and skill in the industry".

Plan for Coal

An important problem with which the Coal Board is faced is the raising of the technical level of the industry. In the autumn of 1950 the Board drew up its plan for the reconstruction of the industry over the next 10 to 15 years. The "Plan for Coal" proposes a "balanced programme of capital development, designed to increase output, improve productivity and reduce costs, by employing men and money where they can produce the best results"[1]. The Minister approved the Plan in October 1951, but emphasized that "the rate at which the Plan is executed, and the amount of investment undertaken each year, must necessarily depend upon decisions taken from time to time by the Government on investment policy, the availability of materials and on employment and social considerations"[2].

The Plan covers the period from 1950 to 1965. It tries to make an estimate of future consumption 15 years hence. The Board estimated that in the period 1961–65 they will be able to dispose of between 230 and 250 million tons of coal a year both at home and abroad. For purposes of simplification, the future demand was placed at a figure of 240 million tons and the Board was conscious that the actual demand may be substantially more or less than 240 million tons.

---

[1] *Plan for Coal* issued by the N.C.B., p. 1.
[2] N.C.B., *Report and Accounts for* 1951, p. 230.

In order to raise the productivity to meet the increased demand, the Board proposes to make a total investment of £ 520 million in the industry. Besides opening up new pits, a considerable portion of the total investment will have to be spent in checking a decline in the output of the existing pits. A sum of £ 350 million will be required for this purpose. Machinery and equipment will have to be maintained and replaced. As time passes, thinner seams will be worked out for getting coal. According to detailed surveys of possibilities of production drawn up by the Board, it is clear that a major portion of the increased future production will have to come from the existing pits. But not all the pits would be kept in production. A number of smaller and uneconomic ones will be closed down or absorbed into more economic units. The miners will be transferred to the nearby pits. In some parts, Cumberland and West Durham for example, social consequences of a sharp reduction in mining employment have been given due consideration. Output will be increased mainly in parts of Scotland, East Durham, Yorkshire, East Midlands, North Staffordshire, South Wales and the small coalfield of Kent. It is hoped that the reconstructed industry will need about 80,000 fewer mineworkers than are employed at present. The Board is determined not to allow a return to the pre-war situation when the industry was over-manned and when a slackness in demand for coal resulted in severe unemployment in the mining areas. The Board wants to have a stable labour force working a five-day week. It is hoped that the reduced labour force will be able to produce about 120% of the present output of coal and thus satisfy the increased future demand.

The Plan shows that the Board has accepted the main recommendations of the Report of the Technical Advisory Committee, 1945. The execution of the Plan will be left in the hands of local management. The Board also realises that the Plan is not meant to be rigid and that it would take into consideration new facts and mining techniques as they come to light with the passage of time.

Summary

The Coal Industry Nationalisation Act was enacted in 1946. On 1st January, 1947, the industry was taken over by a Public

Corporation, the National Coal Board, which was set-up to run the industry. The Board has divided the whole country into nine Divisions. Each Division is operated by a Divisional Board and is responsible for the production of coal within its jurisdiction and for discharging certain other regional functions. The Divisions are sub-divided into 50 Areas and each Area has a number of collieries within its charge. Thus, each colliery is responsible through its Manager to the Area General Manager, the Area through its Area General Manager to the Division, and the Divisional Board is answerable to the N.C.B. The N.C.B. is responsible to the Parliament and the people through the Minister of Fuel and Power. The Minister has the right to give directions of a general character to the N.C.B.

The N.C.B. was charged by the Act to recognize representative workers' organisations for the purpose of discussing with them matters relating to consultation and conciliation. The organisations which have been recognized by the Board are: The National Union of Mineworkers, the British Association of Colliery Management, the National Association of Colliery, Overmen, Deputies and Shotfirers, the Clerical Administrative Workers' Union and the National Association of Clerical and Supervisory Staffs. In case of certain grades of workers, two or more organisations jointly represent the grades concerned.

Conciliation machinery in the industry, with slight modifications, is an extension of what was already in existence before nationalisation. It works at three levels, *viz.*, the National, the District and the Pit. There is a Joint National Negotiating Committee which discusses national questions, and, in case of disagreement, refers them to the National Reference Tribunal. The Tribunal's judgment is final and binding. The whole country has been divided into 18 wage districts, each having a District Conciliation Board and a District Referee. On the pit level, the unsettled question passes through five stages till it reaches the District Umpire whose judgment is final and binding.

The Consultative machinery works through a National Consultative Council, Divisional and Area Consultative Councils and the Pit Consultative Committees. The Consultative Councils and Committees deal with questions of health, safety, welfare arrangement at the colliery and other matters of mutual interest, excluding those which concern wages and conditions of employment. The latter fall within the purview of the Conciliation machinery.

Schemes of welfare in the industry are divided into "Colliery Welfare" and "Social Welfare". The former are the responsibility of the Board and the latter are looked after by a newly created organisation called the Coal Industry Social Welfare Organisation. The Organisation's activities are financed by grants made by the Board from time to time. A Coal Industry Social Welfare Scheme, drawn up in 1952, is executed through nine Divisional Welfare Committees.

Since its inception, the Board has been facing an acute manpower shortage in the industry. The figures for manpower had been showing a decline since 1920 and the trend was aggravated during the war when a number of miners joined the armed forces and took up employments in war-time industries. The Board has been trying to arrest this decline and has sought to achieve this by (i) recruiting Polish and Italian workers, (ii) organizing publicity campaigns, (iii) extending housing and training facilities to new-comers in the industry, (iv) transferring men to more productive pits and (v) working out plans which will enable the Board to make a more effective use of the existing labour force in the industry.

In order to raise the technical level of the industry — a much needed reform — the Board drew up a "Plan for Coal" in 1950, which, by making a balanced programme of capital investment, would raise the productivity in the industry and satisfy the increased demand in the next 10 to 15 years. The Plan is not rigid and will be modified in the light of new experience gained as its execution proceeds.

CHAPTER III

CONFLICT IN COAL-MINING: A GENERAL SURVEY[1]

In this chapter we shall make an attempt to survey the course of conflict in the coal-mining industry after nationalisation. We shall adopt the following treatment. The disputes in each year would be discussed in a general manner. Thus, the number of disputes, the average loss incurred through the smaller disputes, the relative positions of the Divisions in the over-all picture of conflict in Britain and the extent to which the conciliation machinery was utilized before a dispute deteriorated into a stoppage or a restriction — all these will be discussed from year to year. Statistics concerning these problems will be presented in tabular forms[2]. The treatment of such a vast subject will have to be in rather general terms, since, under the searching eye of an analyst, each dispute may have something new to reveal. The frequency of small stoppages and "go-slows", which take place every day in the widely scattered pits of Britain, makes their discussion in a manner approaching completeness an almost impossible task. Part of this task we will try to accomplish in Chapter V. The chapter will end with a summary of the important points which arise from our discussion.

Over-all position of the disputes

Table I below shows the number of stoppages and restrictions, the tonnage lost in each year and the loss represented as a percentage of the annual output for the period 1947–1953.

[1] Part of the material presented in this chapter was collected from the offices of the N.C.B. and the N.U.M. The N.C.B.'s Annual Reports, otherwise excellent documents, give very sketchy information about disputes. The author is, therefore, doubly grateful to the Industrial Relations Department of the Board and the London Office of the N.U.M. for giving him access to the relevant facts and figures.

[2] It may be pointed out here that the statistics issued by the N.C.B. and the Ministry of Labour sometimes differ. The large number of small lightning strikes is probably responsible for this. We have drawn upon both the sources.

TABLE I

Year	No. of stoppages & Restrictions	Tonnage lost	
		Million tons[1]	% of output
1947	1,635	1.7	0.9
1948	1,528	1.1	0.5
1949	1,634	1.5	0.8
1950	1,613	1.0	0.5
1951	1,637	1.1	0.5
1952	2,365	1.9	0.8
1953	2,324	1.1	0.5

Source: *N.C.B. Report* for the years 1952 & 1953

[1] The table above gives "raised and weighed" output and also includes an estimate of tonnage lost through "go-slow" working.

1947. As shown in Table I, during 1947 the total number of stoppages and restrictions was 1635 which resulted in a loss in production of about 1,652,000 tons. There were two important causes which made disputes more frequent in 1947 as compared to 1946[1]. On the 30th June, a ban that restricted changes in wages at particular collieries, and which originated out of a national agreement signed in April 1944 by the Union and Colliery owners[2], was lifted. This was followed by a large number of pent-up demands for revisions in wage-rates which opened a controversial field between the Board and the miners. The second cause was the introduction of the Five-Day Week[3] which resulted in altering the wages of different categories of workers and gave rise to discontent. The Agreement also laid down that "the Union will not countenance any restriction of effort by workmen in failure to perform the work"[4] assessed jointly by the management and the workingmen or the representatives of the two parties. Another factor which led to a number of disputes was Clause 13 of the Agreement which laid down that

[1] The total number of strikes in 1946 was 1,329, vide N.C.B. *Report and Accounts for 1947*, p. 17.

[2] The text of the Agreement can be found in: *N.C.B. Memorandum of Agreements etc.*, Part I, March 20, 1940 to July 31, 1946, pp. 80–98.

[3] The Five-day Week Agreement came into force on May 5, 1947. It provided that the normal working week for underground workers should consist of five consecutive shifts of 7½ hours each plus one winding time. Towards the end of 1947 the increased demand for coal necessitated an extension in working hours. Decisions were to be taken on the local level whether the extension in working hours should be secured by working on Saturdays or by working an extra half-hour from Mondays to Fridays, or both.

[4] *ibid.*, para. 11.

in the event of a workman's normal work not being available, he should perform any alternative work which he is regarded competent to discharge and which is offered to him by the management[1]. Such adjustments created changes in established work-patterns and resulted in disputes. The Durham Winding Enginemen's disputes in May 1947, which involved directly and indirectly 26, 910 enginemen and other workers, caused a loss of 88,681 tons. These disputes arose out of the feeling on the part of Winding Enginemen that the Five-Day Week Agreement would adversely affect their earnings[2]. Though out

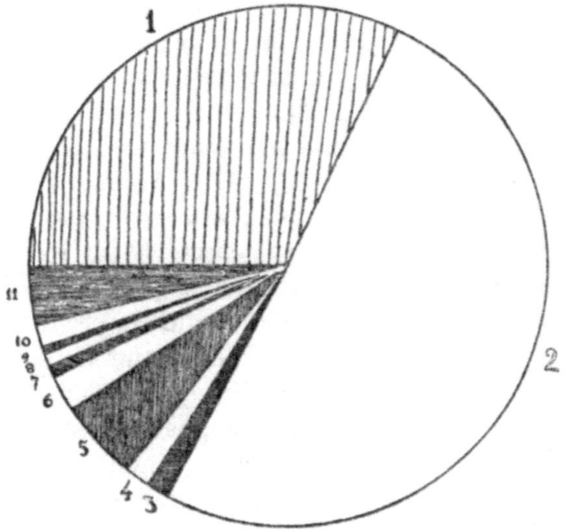

Code figure	*Represents*
1	Dissatisfaction about wages.
2	Application of the terms and conditions of the Five Day Week.
3	Personnel and Grading questions.
4	Working conditions.
5	Methods of working and colliery organisation.
6	Refusal to accept alternative work.
7	Refusal to perform work not completed on a previous shift.
8	Refusal to await repairs after a mechanical breakdown.
9	Objection to, or disputes with, officials.
10	Sympathy with dismissed or suspended workmen.
11	Miscellaneous.

Source: Based on figures given in: N.C.B., *Annual Report and Accounts for 1947.*

[1] *ibid.*, para. 13.
[2] *Ministry of Labour Gazette*, June 1947, p. 207.

of a total number of 1,635 disputes during the year 1947 only 78 arose from the "application of the terms and conditions of the Five-Day Week Agreement", the total loss caused by such disputes was substantial and amounted to about 838,000 tons, constituting more than 50% of the total loss of about 1,652,000 tons in 1947[1].

The circular diagram on the previous page is presented to show the losses caused by different factors, including the application of the Five Day Week Agreement during the year 1947.

The Agreement was arrived at after due deliberations and lengthy discussions, both inside the ranks of the Union and the Board and at the joint meetings of the National Negotiating Committee. In the wider context of the coal supply situation in the country the seriousness of which was summed up in the term "Fuel Crisis", the loss through stoppages became increasingly irritating, both to the Coal Board and to the leaders of the Union. A study of the N.U.M.'s Annual Conference of July 1947 shows that the situation worsened to such an extent that at one time the Coal Board considered the re-introduction of legal proceedings against the strikers for breach of contract, a step which was opposed by the N.U.M. in order to maintain the cordial relations between the Board and the Union[2]. The miners' leaders themselves were becoming conscious of two unpalatable facts: first, that these stoppages, unofficial and unconstitutional, showed no tendency to diminish, and secondly, that by not making use of the comprehensive machinery which existed for the settlement of disputes, the workers, by and large, showed themselves to be unconscious of the responsibility which devolved upon them after nationalisation. In certain parts, as the Coal Board Report for 1947 pointed out, there was a tendency on the part of some men to ignore the conciliation machinery completely.

---

[1] N.C.B., *Annual Report and Accounts for* 1947, p. 17.

[2] Referring to this, *The Economist* supported the idea of prosecuting the strikers. In its issue of July 12, 1947 (p. 56), it wrote: "In an industry where relations between labour and management have such a bad tradition, the Coal Board has hitherto wisely avoided prosecution in the interests of building up good relations. But it is quite clear that some miners are utterly uninterested in good relations or anything else except how to obtain as much money as possible for as little work as possible. In the interests of the majority of miners, let alone the interests of the country, these wreckers should be prosecuted".

There were, during the year under review, four major strikes, which together were responsible for more than 57% of the loss caused by the total number of disputes. Thus, the overwhelming number of strikes or "go-slows", *i.e.*, 1631, resulted in an average loss of about 430 tons each. The most important of them all, the Grimethorpe Dispute, which resulted in a loss of 595,000 tons in output, has been discussed in detail in Chapter V.

Analysing the losses according to Divisions, we find that the largest amount of aggregate loss was incurred in the North-Eastern Division, which was followed by the Scottish, North-Western, Northern and South-Western Divisions. The loss in the North-Eastern Division during the year under review was the heaviest ever experienced in any Division in the industry under nationalisation. The Grimethorpe dispute was an important contributory factor in this direction.

1948. The Year 1948 witnessed 1,528 stoppages and restrictions involving 190,915 men and a total loss of about 1,062,300 tons. The stoppages in the coal-mining industry during the year under review came to about two-thirds of the total number of stoppages in all the industries and were responsible for nearly one quarter of the total time lost[1]. However, only one dispute concerning Shotfirers' wages was of great magnitude involving a loss of 213,045 tons. In addition, there were seven other stoppages or restrictions which caused a loss of 10,000 tons each or over. Total loss in production caused by stoppages in 1948, as compared to 1947, was less by about 590,000 tons. However, the tonnage lost through the smaller stoppages and restrictions increased in 1948 by 96,661[2] tons as compared to 1947. The re-assessment of tasks consequent on the introduction of the Five-Day week continued to create differences between the workers and the management. The New Safety Regulations introduced by the

[1] *Ministry of Labour Gazette*, January 1949, p. 6.
[2] The figure has been arrived at as under:

	1947 (tons)	1948
Total tonnage lost for Britain	1,652,000	1,062,300
less loss involved in Grimethorpe dispute. . . .	595,000	—
	1,057,000	1,062,300
less tonnage lost through other disputes which caused a loss of 10,000 tons or over	405,094	313,733
Loss through smaller disputes	651,906	748,567

Excess of tonnage lost through smaller disputes in 1948 over 1947 = 96,661 t.

Minister of Fuel and Power in 1947 also brought about readjustments in the amount of work performed by certain classes of workers. Besides, a National Agreement about the wages of craftsmen left the grading to be settled locally. Another Agreement, which was concluded at the end of 1947 concerning the wages and conditions of "weekly-paid" industrial staff, provided for wages to be reviewed locally. A further difficulty arose when agreements conferring benefits on shotfirers and winding enginemen raised the question whether certain grades of workers could or could not be included in the classes which were covered by those agreements[1].

Analysing the disputes by causes, we find that in 1948 wages, price lists, allowances and bonuses were responsible for 631 out of a total of 1,528 disputes (about 42 %), invloving a loss of 643,900 tons out of a total loss of 1,062,300 tons (about 61 %)[2]. "Methods of working and colliery organisation" came second, gave rise to 290 disputes and caused a loss of 182,000 tons in output, a fact which showed that the technical reorganisation of the industry had begun to create tensions between the workers and the Board[3]. The application of the Five-Day week agreement gave rise to 8 disputes and resulted in a loss of 15,200 tons in output. The Board also resorted to legal action against the strikers for breach of contract; actually there was a protest strike in Ayrshire against the Court Award for breach of contract arising out of a strike at another colliery which resulted in a loss of 23,830 tons.

On the Divisional basis, in the year 1948 the Scottish, North-Eastern and South-Eastern Divisions recorded increased losses in output as compared to the year 1947, while the Northern, North-Western, West Midlands and South-Western Divisions recorded significant decreases in losses caused by disputes. The largest amount of loss was recorded in the North-Eastern Division, followed by the Scottish Division.

1949. The year 1949 recorded a total number of 1,634 stoppages

[1] N.C.B., *Report and Accounts for* 1948, p. 35.
[2] *ibid.*, p. 36.
[3] For some of the problems of reorganisation of the industry *vis-a-vis* industrial conflict, see the discussion of the two disputes, *viz.*, the Grimethorpe Dispute of 1947 and the Protest strike against the closure of Wern Tarw Colliery of June 1951, Chapter V.

and restrictions and resulted in a loss of about 1,543,000 tons. About 60% of the loss was caused by four big disputes[1]. In 1947, the major stoppages caused about 58% of the aggregate loss, while in 1948 the figure was about 29%. The smaller disputes, i.e., those which resulted in a loss of less than ten thousand tons in output, were numerous and constituted about 99% of the total number of disputes that occurred during the year 1949, but the total loss arising out of the smaller disputes came to only about 39% of the total loss in the industry. Thus, the average loss of the smaller types of disputes came to about 400 tons each, slightly less than the figure recorded in 1947. The Concessionary Coal Dispute, which incurred the greatest amount of loss during the year, *viz.*, 382,590 tons, involved about 44,000 colliery workers and led to a loss of about 250,000 working days[2]. The demand for an increase in wages by Colliery Winding Enginemen in Yorkshire and Lancashire led to a stoppage towards the end of August, affected 90,000 workers and resulted in a loss of approximately 230,000 working days[3]. A demand for higher wages by nearly 12,000 oncost and other workers at various coalfields in Scotland resulted in a loss of about 50,000 working days and about 80,000 tons of coal[4].

If we leave out of account the Concessionary Coal Dispute, "dissatisfaction with bonuses, allowances, wages and price lists" caused during the year under review a total loss of 865,000 tons (about 56% of the aggregate loss); "methods of working and colliery organisation", a loss of 128,000 tons (about 8%); "working conditions", 63,000 tons (about 4%)[5]; and "refusal to accept alternative work" and "sympathy with men dismissed or suspended" about 18,000 tons each (1%)[6].

[1] The four disputes referred to were as follows:
i) Oncost workers protest stoppage in Scotland (September);
ii) Winding Enginemen's claim for higher wage rate in North-Eastern Division (August);
iii) Concessionary Coal Claim for Lancashire (May); and
iv) Winding Enginemen's Claim for higher wage rate in North-Western Division (August).

[2] See Chapter V.

[3] *Ministry of Labour Gazette*, May 1950, p. 158.

[4] *ibid.*, and *N.C.B. Annual Report*, 1949, p. 83.

[5] In the South-Western Division, a number of stoppages took place because of the alleged failure to carry out adequate dust suppression by infusion methods.

[6] N.C.B., *Report and Accounts for 1949*, p. 82.

On the Divisional level, the Scottish, Northern (N & C), North-Western, West Midlands and South-Western Divisions showed increased losses as compared to the year 1948, and the remaining Divisions showed decreases. The greatest increase was recorded in the North-Western Division, which was caused by the Concessionary Coal Claim and the Winding Enginemen's claim for higher wage rate, both of which together resulted in a loss of 443,755 tons. While the stoppages beginning in the year 1949 in the coal-mining industry came to 61.2 % of the total stoppages taking place in the same year in all the industries, thus showing a slight decrease over the figure for 1948, the percentage of workers at 57 % and the working days lost at 41.7 % showed an increase over the 1948 figures when these stood at 44.3 and 22.3 % respectively. The Coal Board since the year 1949 started making a tabular analysis of the percentage of stoppages and restrictions in each Division in relation to the conciliation machinery. According to information gathered from the records in the office of the Coal Board, which we have shown in Table V, we find that during 1949 in Britain as a whole about 4.8 % of the stoppages and restrictions in coal-mining took place without any reference to the conciliation machinery. In about 40 % of the disputes, the conciliation machinery was used only up to the first stage, while in about 32 % the stoppage or restriction of effort started after discussions had taken place between men and manager (*i.e.*, the second stage). Only in 7 % and 6 % of the cases, the conciliation machinery was fairly exhausted (till the 9th and 10th stages respectively) before the dispute resulted in stoppage or restriction. The North-Western Division was significant in this respect inasmuch as about 51 % and 11 % of the disputes reached the stage of discussions at the national level. It may be pointed out once again that this Division recorded the Concessionary Coal and the Winding Enginemen's disputes. Some other general remarks on the position of the Divisions individually in regard to the utilization of the conciliation machinery can be summed up as follows: most of the disputes were carried up to the second stage of conciliation and thereafter it appears that no serious effort was made to take advantage of the disputes-settlement machinery which exists in the industry, a fact which indicates that despite the existence of comprehensive machinery which seeks to settle differences through methods of consultation and conciliation, the workers on their part showed little recognition of this fact and relied on strikes, rather than on peaceful methods, for the settlement of their grievances.

1950. As shown in Table I, the year 1950 recorded a total number of 1,613 stoppages and restrictions and caused a loss in output of about a million tons, the lowest during the period 1947–50. The highest amount of loss occurred in the Scottish Division. Some 170,000 days were lost by over 26,000 workers during July at various Scottish collieries in support of a demand for increase in the wages of lower paid workers. In September and the beginning of October, further strikes took place because of the alleged delay in the settlement of disputes, resulting in a loss of about 25,000 working days and involving more than 8000 workers. The matter was finally referred to the National Reference Tribunal with whose judgment the workers expressed dissatisfaction. They staged another protest strike in the beginning of November, which affected about 10,000 workers and resulted in a loss of about 32,000 working days[1]. These four disputes caused a loss in output of 336,100 tons, which was about 33% of the total loss caused by all the disputes in the industry in the year under review. If we take out the nine disputes that caused a loss of 10,000 tons or over, we find that 1604 disputes caused a total loss of 635,772 tons thus giving an average loss of about 400 tons each. Thus the average loss from the smaller type of disputes had remained fairly uniform over the past years in the industry under nationalisation. From Table II, which shows the losses in different years according to each cause, we find that as compared to 1949, the amount of coal lost in 1950 as a result of disputes arising out of "questions of wages and price lists", "methods of working and colliery organisation" and "allowances and bonuses" had gone down. But as a percentage of the total loss, there had been an all-round increase in 1950 in the losses due to different causes as compared to the year 1949, when the Concessionary Coal Dispute alone was responsible for about

[1] *Ministry of Labour Gazette*, May 1951, p. 188.

24.8% of the total loss. As a percentage of the total stoppages, of workers involved and working days lost in all the industries in Britain in 1950, the coal-mining industry accounted for 64.2%, 46.8% and 31% respectively; the figures for 1949, as we have already seen, were 61.2, 57 and 41.7% respectively (Table III).

The Scottish Division accounted for the highest amount of loss. In all other Divisions the amount of losses incurred had been very much less than the previous three years, except in the Scottish and South-Eastern Divisions. The figure for the latter in 1950 went up to 47,000 tons as against 17,000 tons in 1949 and in the North-Western Division also the figure was higher as compared to the loss incurred in 1948.

The recourse to conciliation for the settlement of disputes showed a decline and it is estimated that about 12% of the stoppages or restrictions took place without any reference to the legalised means which exist in the industry for the settlement of disputes. This compares unfavourably with the record of the year 1949 when the percentage of stoppages and restrictions which were not referred to the conciliation machinery at all was 4.8. The increase in 1950 over 1949 was due mainly to the stoppages of the oncost workers in Scotland. Thus, in Scotland about 21.6% of disputes deteriorated into stoppages and restrictions of effort without any reference to the conciliation machinery. The majority of disputes reached only the first and second stages. Only in a little more than 2% the ninth and eleventh stages were reached, *i.e.*, the disputes were discussed at the National Conciliation Board and referred to the National Reference Tribunal. Thus the results of the year 1950 also showed that there was no serious effort on the part of the workers to utilize the existing conciliation arrangements.

1951. A total number of 1,637 stoppages and restrictions in the year 1951 caused a loss of about 1,113,000 tons which came to about 0.5 per cent of the raised and weighed output. This was about 73,000 tons more than the loss incurred during the year 1950 and about 51,000 tons higher than in 1948. Expressed as a percentage of the total loss, the figure for 1951 remained the same as in 1950 and 1948 and was less than the years 1947 and

1949 (Table I). The increase in the year 1951 over 1950 was caused mainly by two factors. First, there was an increased loss through restrictions, and, secondly, there was an extensive stoppage in the South Western Division as a protest against the closure of Wern Tarw Colliery which rendered 29 collieries and 2 central washeries idle in sympathy. This stoppage was the biggest of the year and resulted in a loss in output of about 115,177 tons[1]. From Table III we find that, expressed as a percentage of the number of stoppages, workers involved and working days lost in all the industries in Britain during the year 1951, coal-mining was responsible for 61.4, 35.8 and 20.6 respectively, an all-round decrease as compared to the year 1950[2].

Table II adapted from the National Coal Board Report for 1951 shows the amount of loss according to each cause expressed as a percentage of the total loss incurred through disputes during the years 1947–1951.

The largest percentage of loss, about 51.7, was caused, as in all the previous years (except 1947, where 50.1 % of the loss was classified as having arisen from the "Conditions of Five-Day Week Agreement), by "Wages and price lists"; "methods of working and colliery organisation" came second with 20.7 %, followed by "allowances and bounses" which were responsible for 6.6 % of the total loss. Compared to the year 1950, the losses in 1951 through items 1, 4 and 5 showed decreased percentages, while items 2, 3, 6, 7, 8 and 9 showed increased percentages; item 10, *viz.*, "refusal to await repairs" remained the same in both the years. The loss caused by "sympathy with men dismissed or suspended" came to 3.1 % and thus became the largest over the period 1947–1951. The largest amount of loss arising from this factor was in the Scottish Division where numerous dismissals took place and men staged sympathetic strikes.

Out of a total number of 1,637 stoppages and restrictions, there were 13 which caused a loss of 10,000 tons or over and resulted in a total loss of 285,819 tons in output. Thus the smaller stoppages and restrictions numbered 1,624 and involved a loss of about 814,181 tons, thus averaging a loss of a little over

[1] See Chapter V.
[2] Also, *Ministry of Labour Gazette*, May 1951, p. 166.

TABLE II

Causes	1947 Loss in thousand tons	% of total loss	1948 Loss in thousand tons	% of total loss	1949 Loss in thousand tons	% of total loss	1950 Loss in thousand tons	% of total loss	1951 Loss in thousand tons	% of total loss
1. Wages and Price-lists	493	29.8	585	55.0	813	52.7	702	67.5	575	51.7
2. Methods of working and colliery organisation	80	4.8	182	17.1	128	8.3	104	10	230	20.7
3. Allowances and bonuses	42	2.5	59	5.6	52	3.4	51	4.9	74	6.6
4. Working conditions	25	1.5	44	4.1	63	4.1	55	5.3	50	4.5
5. Alternative work	37	2.2	23	2.2	18	1.2	36	3.5	36	3.2
6. Sympathy with men dismissed or suspended	22	1.3	24	2.3	17	1.1	15	1.4	34	3.1
7. Personnel and grading questions	26	1.6	13	1.2	11	.7	15	1.4	24	2.2
8. Work left over from previous shift	11	0.7	8	0.8	8	.5	7	.6	26	2.3
9. Objections to or disputes with officials	8	0.5	13	1.2	12	.7	5	.5	14	1.3
10. Refusal to await repairs	12	0.7	11	1.0	8	.5	10	.9	10	.9
11. Conditions of five-day week Agreement	838	50.1	15	1.4	—	—	—	—	—	—
12. Concessionary Coal	—	—	—	—	383	24.8	—	—	—	—
13. Miscellaneous	60	3.6	85	8.0	30	1.9	40	3.8	40	3.6

Note: The Table above gives "raised and weighed" output and includes an estimate of tonnage lost through "go-slow" working.

500 tons from each such dispute. This showed an increase in the average amount lost through smaller disputes as compared to the years before 1951.

About half the collieries in the year 1951 were free from strikes and "go-slows". On the Divisional level, the largest amount of loss through disputes was recorded in the North-Eastern Division where about 278,000 tons were lost compared to 803,000 tons, which was the total saleable tonnage lost in the country in that year; Scotland accounted for about 253,000 tons followed by the South-Western Division with about 151,000 tons. Compared to the year 1950, the Northern (N & C), North-Eastern, East Midlands and South-Western Divisions showed increased losses during the year under review, while Scotland, Durham, North-Western, West Midlands and South-Eastern Divisions showed decreased losses. Thus, like most of the previous years, the three Divisons, namely, Scottish, North-Eastern and South-Western continued to show great losses.

The percentage of disputes resulting in stoppages or "go-slows" without reference to the conciliation machinery dropped from 11.6 % in 1950 and 4.8 % in 1949 to 2.7 % in 1951 (Table V). The large majority of disputes, before finally deteriorating into stoppages or "go-slows", reached only the first and second stages, while only in an insignificant percentage of the disputes, *viz.*, 0.1 %, genuine efforts seemed to have been made for exhausting the possibility of conciliation for the settlement of disputes. It would be correct to say that the tendency to ignore the conciliation machinery for reconciling the differences continued during the year 1951.

1952. During the year 1952, 2,365 stoppages and restrictions were recorded which involved a total loss of about 1.9 million tons in output, the highest that had ever been experienced in the coal-mining industry under nationalisation. Expressed as a percentage of the total output, it came to 0.8 per cent. The comparatively large quantity of coal lost during the year under review was caused mainly by three major strikes or series of strikes, *viz.*, the protest action involving stoppages and ban on Saturday working against the 24th Award of the National

Reference Tribunal[1], causing losses that were estimated at 61,035 tons in the Scottish, and 160,269 tons in the South-Western, Divisions[2]; the Overmen, Deputies and Shotfirers strike at 18 collieries in the North-Eastern Division owing to dissatisfaction with progress of negotiations for a wage increase resulting in a loss of 73,130 tons; and finally, the strike of Winding Enginemen in December in the North-Eastern Division caused by the demand for an increase in wages, which resulted in a loss of 214,091 tons. The Winders in Yorkshire claimed that the wages of Enginemen in a neighbouring coalfield had been raised and that a similar increase should have been given to those working in Yorkshire, and in support of this demand a strike was staged. The claim was rejected by the Board and normal work was resumed after a few days[3]. According to the *Ministry of Labour Gazette*, the dispute resulted in a loss of about 105,000 working days and involved about 45,800 men.

The number of strikes which caused a loss of 10,000 tons or over was 19 and as a consequence of these alone about 879,797 tons of coal was lost. Thus the remaining 2,346 disputes resulted in a loss of about 1,020,203 tons, giving an average loss of about 430 tons each from small disputes. In the year 1952, the coal-mining industry accounted for about one-third of the aggregate time lost through stoppages in 1952 and thus became responsible for the greatest loss of time during the year[4]. From Table III, we find that expressed as a percentage of stoppages, of workers involved and working days lost in all the industries in Britain in the year 1952, the coal-mining industry accounted for 71.2, 65.7 and 36.8 per cent respectively. While the first two figures were the highest so far recorded, the figure of 36.8 % was less than the figures for the years 1947 and 1949 which were 37.4 and 41.7 % respectively.

Analysing the disputes by causes[5], we find that the losses caused by "Wages, price lists and allowances" increased from

[1] See Chapter V.

[2] This factor was also responsible, in the case of South-Western Division, for a loss of 34,090 tons in output in 1953.

[3] N.C.B. *Annual Report and Accounts for 1952*, p. 53.

[4] *Ministry of Labour Gazette*, May 1953, p. 152.

[5] The Coal Board's Annual Reports for 1952 and 1953, unlike the previous Reports, do not give the analysis of disputes according to causes. Our analysis is based on the information collected from the N.C.B.'s office, London.

58.3% in 1951 to about 75% in 1952, the highest percentage ever recorded during the five years of nationalisation. Besides the three major disputes which swelled the figure, there were minor demands for wage increases and for stabilisation of piece-work prices and allowances for abnormal conditions. The loss caused by "working conditions and colliery organisation" in 1952 showed a decline over the figures for the year 1951. A number of disputes were caused by such factors as the measuring of face advance, refusal by the manager to allow a number of miners, who were being paid allowances for working in water, to leave the pit early, inadequate supply of tubs, etc. One of such disputes in the South-Western Division at Bwllfa and 8 other collieries resulted in a loss of 32,380 tons. There was one dispute about the removal of the under-manager causing a loss of about 10,610 tons, and another in sympathy with a worker who was suspended for refusing to obey an order, which involved a loss of 41,695 tons.

In the year 1952 the largest amount of loss through stoppages and restrictions was incurred in the North-Eastern Division and came to about 642,000 tons. The North-Eastern Division has been responsible for the greatest amount of aggregate loss over the years 1947–1953. As we have already said, the two important disputes, *viz.*, the Winding Enginemen's and the Overmen, Deputies and Shotfirers Disputes occurred in this Division, besides several other disputes which resulted in substantial losses. Scotland came next with an approximate loss of 375,000 tons, followed by the South-Western Division which recorded a figure of about 221,000 tons. With the exception of North-Western and East Midlands Divisions, all other Divisions recorded increased losses in 1952 as compared to the year1951.

With regard to the use of the conciliation machinery, the figures for the year 1952, as mentioned in Table V, reveal no significant change as compared to the previous years. 6.4% of the disputes resulted in stoppages or "go-slows" without being referred to the conciliation machinery; the large percentage of disputes, *i.e.*, 28.6 and 39.8% reached only the first and second stages. The figure of 11.1% shown in column 10 in Table V refers to the protest action involving stoppages against the 24th Award of the National Reference Tribunal. Thus the conclusion which can be drawn from the results of the year 1952 confirms what has already been said that the miners generally strike or take "go-slow" action without a proper utilisation of the dispute-settlement machinery which exists in the industry.

1953. The figure of 2,324 stoppages and restrictions in the year 1953 was, with the exception of 1952, higher than any other previous year. The tonnage of coal lost through disputes was 1.15 million tons, and, as compared to the loss in 1952, was less by about 560,000 tons[1]. The reason for this diminuition was the absence of any major disputes of the size of those recorded in 1952, when, as we have already shown, a substantial loss was incurred through the incidence of a comparatively fewer number of disputes. The number of disputes which caused a loss of ten thousand tons or over was 9. The greatest loss was occasioned by a dispute during the early part of the year by the continuance of "ban on Saturday working due to general dissatisfaction with wages following the 24th Porter Award" in the South-Western Division, which resulted in a loss of about 34,090 tons in output. Another equally big loss amounting to about 33,550 tons arose out of a dispute concerning the conversion of a part production face into a fully reserved training face, which, it was claimed by the miners, would have involved the transfer of a small number of workers at lower pay. About 27,000 working days were lost by about 2,800 workers in this dispute[2]. Expressed as a percentage of the total output, the figure of loss for the year 1953 was 0.5. It was less than the figures for the years 1947, 1949 and 1952 and was equal to that of 1948, 1950 and 1951 (Table I). The disputes which caused a loss of less than 10,000 tons, numbering 2,315, resulted in a total loss of 991,723 tons. Thus the average loss arising out of smaller disputes came to about 430 tons, and showed no change as compared to the figure for 1952.

Analysing the disputes by causes, we find that the largest loss of tonnage in 1953 arose, as in most previous years, by disputes concerning "wages, price lists and allowances" and totalled about 64% of the aggregate loss in the industry. There

[1] N.C.B., *Annual Report and Accounts for* 1953, p. 14.
[2] *Ministry of Labour Gazette*, May 1954, p. 151.

was an increase in disputes caused by the "payment of allowances" for such things as waiting-time, working in wet or cold conditions. The loss in output caused by disputes due to general organisation and working conditions showed an increase over the year 1952 and was estimated at 26% of the aggregate loss. Working arrangements at the face or surface, early finishing, wet conditions of roof and similar other factors increased the number of disputes under the classifications of "methods of working and colliery organisation" and "working conditions".

In the wider set-up of the disputes in all the industries in Britain during the period under discussion, we find that coal-mining was again responsible for the largest number of stoppages. Thus, the figures in coal-mining, shown as a percentage of stoppages, workers involved and working days lost in all industries in 1953, were 74.8, 12.2 and 18 respectively. Compared to the figures for 1952, the percentage of stoppages in 1953 increased from 71.2 to 74.8, the figures of workers involved and working days lost showed considerable decline from 65.7 to 12.2 and 36.8 to 18% respectively (Table III). This state of affairs was caused by the absence of big and long drawn-out battles between the Coal Board and the workers during the year 1953.

The three Divisions of Scotland, North-Eastern and South-Western showed the highest figures of loss through disputes. But, with the exception of West Midlands, all other Divisions showed a decline as compared to the losses which arose in the year 1952 and even the increase in West-Midlands was not very great. The Durham and North-Western Divisions showed the lowest figures of losses in their history since the year 1947.

The use of the conciliation machinery for the settlement of disputes in the year 1953 showed no marked change from the results of the previous years (Table V). 8.6% of the disputes were not referred to the conciliation machinery at all before they resulted in stoppages or restrictions. A major portion of the disputes reached only the first and second stages, while only 5.3% came before the National Reference Tribunal. Compared to the year 1952, the percentage of stoppages and restrictions which did not touch the conciliation machinery at any level in 1953 increased from 6.4 to 8.3. A larger number of stoppages or restrictions also took place after there had been discussions between men and pit officials (first stage) and the increase, over 1952, was from 28.6 to 42.5%. The figures for the second stage showed a decline and in others until the sixth stage there were no significant changes. The comparatively larger figure in column 10 (dispute referred to National Reference Tribunal) in 1952, as has already been pointed out, was caused by the submission of the claim for a general rise in wages to the National Reference Tribunal. Once again, the conciliation machinery was generally ignored and no sustained efforts were made to settle the disputes through the normal channels which had been provided for in the industry.

We have so far attempted to give an over-all picture of the course of conflict in the industry during the years 1947–1953. We shall now focus our attention on some problems connected with disputes.

Causes

General Remarks. Before discussing the causes of strikes in coal-mining, it would be useful to indicate briefly and in broad terms the causes which lead to industrial conflict[1].

One of the most hotly contested areas in the field of industrial relations is the wage-issue and a large number of disputes stem from this source. It is generally agreed by writers on labour problems that wage-fixing is by far the most difficult aspect of the relationship between the employers and the workers. It must, however, be remarked that while in many cases the wage-issue becomes the overt cause, the more fundamental and deep-seated factors lie concealed and sometimes may not have anything to do with wages at all. In such cases, the alleviation of the more immediate grievance, *i.e.*, adjustment of wages, would only result in a temporary postponement of the dispute, and not eradicate the deeper causes without which a lasting settlement would be impossible. Warner and Low found in their investigations that while most of the formal demands of the strikers

[1] For a detailed discussion of this problem, see: K. G. J. C. Knowles, *Strikes, A Study in Industrial Conflict*, Basil Blackwell, 1952, Chapter IV.
Also Knowles' classification into (a) Immediate Causes, (b) Conditioning Causes, and (c) Underlying Causes in "'Strike-Proneness' and its Determinants" (mimeographed), International Sociological Association, Liege Congress, 24 August–1 September, 1953.

concerned questions of wages and the recognition of the trade union, further investigations revealed that actually the basic grounds for the strikes had little to do with wages[1]. Thus, the frequency of wage-disputes "means no more than that a high proportion of the strikes took the *form* of wage strikes. Since wages stand for more than can be bought with them, wages tend to be symbolic of wider grievances"[2]. The reason why most of the disputes are given the colour of a wage-issue is that "in any conflict situation, effective strategy requires that primary issues be given first place and secondary issues be subordinated"[3].

One of the factors which tends to lessen the number of strikes caused by the wage-factor is the increasingly significant role played by political considerations in the relations between the employers and the workers. The labour movement, particularly in Britain, has developed in close association with the Labour Party[4]. The traditional view of industrial relations, however, dit not take the political factor of power and prestige into consideration, and the analyses of disputes tended to lean too heavily on economic factors alone. "If we were forced to decide", writes Ross, "whether the economic or the political aspect of industrial relations is the more crucial, there would be weighty arguments on the side of the political aspect"[5].

A second factor which might lessen conflict stemming from the wage-issue is the increasing respect which is gradually being extended to the system of collective bargaining conducted through joint negotiating bodies. It indicates two important things. First, it shows the increased prestige which the labour unions have come to acquire in the modern society, wherein the employers

---

[1] *The Social System of the Modern Factory*, New Haven, Yale University Press, 1947, p. 131.
Also see, T. T. Paterson and F. J. Willett, "Unofficial Strike", *Sociological Review*, Vol. XLIII, Sec. 4, 1951.

[2] Knowles, *Strikes*, *op. cit.*, p. 219.

[3] A. M. Ross, *Trade Union Wage Policy*, University of California Press, 1950, p. 100.

[4] On this aspect, see: Allan Flanders, *Trade Unions*, H.U.L. 1952, Chap. VII; N. Barou, *British Trade Unions*, Victor Gollancz, 1947, Chap. X; G. D. H. Cole, *An Introduction to Trade Unionism*, George Allen & Unwin Ltd., 1953, Chap. VIII.

[5] Ross, *op. cit.*, also see: Peter F. Drucker, *The New Society — The Anatomy of the Industrial Order*, Harper & Brothers, 1950, Chaps. 7 and 12.
For an opposite view, see John T. Dunlop, *Wage Determination Under Trade Unions*, Basil Blackwell, 1950, pp. iii–vi.

agree, many of them reluctantly still, to sit round a table with the representatives of the workers to settle wage rates and other problems affecting the workers in the industry; secondly, it shows the mutual desire of the two parties to settle the differences by peaceful means rather than indulge in long drawn-out battles to the great detriment of the industry and the community at large. It is a significant change and a great stride forward in the right direction from the times when the decisions on wages, working conditions etc., were regarded to be the inviolable rights of the employers, to the present day when joint consultation is effectively giving to the workers a say in the running of the industry. But it would be wrong to assume that we are anywhere near the solution of the problem of industrial conflict. The institution of joint consultation has opened out before us a long vista of opportunities for the peaceful settlement of industrial disputes. But it is important to note that the establishment of joint negotiating machinery is not of itself a guarantee against industrial unrest. Much depends upon the spirit in which it is worked. In an industry whose history of industrial relations has been full of disputes, like British coal-mining, the unpleasant flavour of mutual antagonism will take considerable time to disappear.

We started out by assessing the share of the wage-factor in causing disputes and then tried to show that (i) in many cases the wage-factor is not the real cause of the dispute, and (ii) that the number of disputes stemming from this source might decrease. However, we should not be understood to imply that all disputes classified as arising from the issue of wages do not have anything to do with discontentment caused by wages. Often the causes of a single dispute are many and varied, and in the absence of any objective yardstick, the relative proportions of different factors joining into one broad complex grievance are impossible to ascertain. It seems true to say, however, that wages still loom large in the psychology of the labour leaders and the rank-and-file of the unions. The intricacy and the large number of the problems involved in the settlement of wages provide ample ground for differences between the workers and the employers. Demands for wage increases, or during adverse times, resistance against cuts in existing levels of wages, remain the most frequent sources of discontent among the workers. Sometimes both these claims can be involved in a single dispute. Thus, in coal-mining when on 1st February 1916 an adjustment of wages fell due, the Conciliation Board was faced by the South-Wales Miners' Federation's claim for a wage advance of 5 per cent, while the coal-owners brought a counter claim for a wage reduction of $3\frac{3}{4}$ per cent. Both these claims were said to be based on economic considerations of the industry[1]. Oftentimes claims are made for equalization of wages in one bargaining unit with the rates in other "comparable" units. "Equal pay for equal work" is a slogan, which though apparently simple and logical, involves a number of difficulties in its practical application. Uniformity in the content of job classifications, methods of wage payment, regularity of employment, all have to be considered while contemplating equalisation of wages. A claim often insisted upon by the labour unions is the demand for an increase in wages parallel with a rise in productivity in the industry. This problem also entails a number of difficulties. Productivity in the different departments of an industry might vary considerably and continued increases in the department which shows constantly rising rates of productivity will have an influence on workers employed in other departments. In the economic structure of a country as a whole, the extractive industries are likely to register smaller increases than those in which a rise in productivity can be made a comparatively easier affair through efficiency techniques. Besides, constant adjustments with the changes in the cost-of-living provide another source of friction between the employers and the workers[2]. Writing about the United States, Millis and Montogomery say: "The median for the percentages of cases in which this (wages) issue entered was 71.7 for the period 1881–1885; 52.5 for 1886–1890; 53.6 for 1891–1895; 55.6 for 1895–1900; 40.9 for 1901–1905; 66.0 for 1916–1920; 52.2 for 1921–1925; 47.5 for 1926–1930; 61.3 for 1931–1935; 49.2 for 1936–1940"[3].

A factor which needs mention here, because it is generally

[1] G. D. H. Cole, *Labour in the Coal-Mining Industry* (1914–1921), Publications of the Carnegie Endowment for International House, 1923, p. 42.

[2] See, Dunlop and Healy, *Collective Bargaining, Principles and Cases*, Richard D. Irwin, Inc., Illinois, 1953, pp. 86–99.

[3] *Organized Labour*, Vol. III, McGraw-Hill Book Co., 1945, p. 699.

forgotten in discussions on wage-issues, is the fact that the wages should be adequate both economically and psychologically. "A wage rate is psychologically inadequate, no matter how large in absolute amount", write Krech and Crutchfield, "if it results in a wide discrepancy between the worker's level of aspiration and his level of achievement"[1]. Each increase in wages, by raising the socio-economic standard of the worker, induces new needs. In other words, it helps in the transformation of "unconscious" into "conscious" wants. Pegging the wages to the cost-of-living alone, therefore, would provide an incomplete solution of the problem. A more dynamic approach, which takes into consideration the spiralling structure of the wants, will reduce the tension amongst the workers and help in avoiding conflict in the industries.

Another factor which causes disputes, and which figured prominently in the early days of the rise of the trade unions, is the employers' resistance to accede to the workers' right to organize themselves. The history of the trade union movement is full of numerous battles it has fought with employers and governments of the day to get itself recognized as spokesman of the workers. Thus in Britain the two important causes of the strikes and lock-outs for the twelve years before the beginning of the first World War "were either economic demands for better wages and conditions, or arose from the pressing forward of organisation too fast in the idea that organisation, however obtained, was necessary to obtain economic improvement"[2]. Often more than one union has existed in the same plant or industry and inter-union fights have been numerous. The employers sometimes regarded these conflicts as internal matters of the union, unless the union insisted on having a right of closed-shop in the industry. Thus to quote Lord Askwith:

> In their eagerness for organisation many trades, especially the miners, struck on the non-union question, which

[1] *Theory and Problems of Social Psychology*, McGraw-Hill Book Co., 1948, p. 542.

[2] Lord Askwith, *Industrial Problems and Disputes*, London, John Murray, 1920, p. 350.

Also: Knowles, *Strikes*, *op. cit.*, pp. 236–37. While even today the recognition of trade unions is not universal outside nationalised industries, "strikes on 'Trade Union principle' are changing their character, and are no longer strikes for the right to organize or for recognition so much as strikes concerned with the closed shop".

> employers regarded as a question outside their scope of action and as one to be decided between workpeople; or only within their scope of action if it was claimed that they were to be compelled to bring non-unionists into a union or not to be allowed to employ any suitable man offering himself for employment. In their eagerness, too, on the same principle, union fought union, while the employers had to suffer passively, in some instances at very heavy cost[1].

The growth of massive industrial unions[2], however, gradually tends to lessen inter-union conflicts, though to say that such disputes have disappeared completely would be an overstatement.

An important socio-psychological consequence of the growth of big workers' organisations, bearing on the problem of industrial conflict, shows itself in deepening "the depersonalization of worker-management contacts". The worker generally presents his grievances, not to the management, but to the union of which he is a member. The unions, in trying to meet the diverse needs of the workers, organize a number of subsidiary activities, *e.g.*, recreation clubs, educational courses, cooperatives. All this tends to "encourage the emerging of genuine psychological groups among workers[3]" and widens the gulf between the workers and the management.

Another important cause of tensions in the industry is the rapid introduction of technical innovations in the production methods. New production methods inevitably affect the set of social relations within which the worker is placed. They bring about changes in size and composition of work team, modify the nature of the contact of the worker with his associates and affect the status of the worker in the organisation. All these changes call for an effort on the part of the worker to adjust himself to the new set of conditions. If the pace of technological changes is fast, it may subject the worker to severe psychological strains[4]. In

---

[1] *ibid.*, p. 351.

[2] On Industrial Unionism, its growth and future prospects, see: N. Barou, *op. cit.*, pp. 23–26; J. D. M. Bell, *Industrial Unionism: A Critical Analysis*, University of Glasgow, 1949; G. D. H. Cole, *An Introduction to Trade Unionism*, Allen & Unwin, 1953, pp. 81–85.

A discussion of inter-union problems in nationalised industries of Britain can be found in the Action Society Trust Pamphlet, *The Future of Unions*, 1951.

[3] Krech and Crutchfield, *op. cit.*, p. 537.

[4] R.K. Merton, *Social Theory and Social Structure*, The Free Press of Glencoe, Illinois, 1951, p. 318.

addition, as Merton suggests, technological changes may also affect the workers in three other ways. First, a technical innovation may render obsolescent the skill of a worker which he may have acquired after putting in long and sustained spells of work. He is called upon to learn new techniques and his sense of personal worth and self-esteem, which is generally associated with his now-obsolescent skill, is threatened. Secondly, the minute division of labour, which is an important element in modern methods of production, tends to reduce the worker to a mere cog in the big industrial wheel. The extremely narrow specialization requires "great imagination on the part of the worker to visualize the finished product to which he contributes, and a great act of will to feel any sense of pride in the product and in participating in its making"[1]. Thirdly, the greater specialization of production calls for a more uniform and predictable behaviour from the workers. The range of individual variations from the standardized pattern of expectations has to be narrowed down by subjecting the workers to an increasingly rigid discipline. This, "under specified conditions, becomes coercive for the worker". In short, the factors which cause frustration amongst the workers are many and varied. One of the ways in which frustration reaction shows itself is the method of strike.

The above brief description of the important causes of strikes does less than justice to the highly complex amalgam of hard economic realities and vague emotions and sentiments which mingle freely in the causation of a dispute. For our purposes, however, we need not enter into details. Bad working conditions, grievances against the foremen, the course of the business cycle, and the underlying sense of inferiority bred into the workers because of their subordinate position in the social structure, the "insecurity neurosis" of the unions, and many other factors have their influence, more or less, on the origin of disputes.

Against the background of these general remarks, we will consider the case of coal-mining. The propensity of the miners

---

[1] J. F. Scott and R. P. Lynton, *The Community Factor in Modern Technology — An International Study of the "Sense of Belonging" in Industry*, U.N.E.S.C.O., Tensions and Technology Series, 1950, p. 113.

TABLE III

Source: *Ministry of Labour Gazette*, 1946–1954

Year	Stoppages beginning in the Year		Workers involved in stoppages in progress		Working days lost through stoppages in progress	
	In coal-mining	In all other industries	In coal-mining	In all other industries	In coal-mining	In all other industries
1947	61.1	38.9	49.4	50.6	37.4	62.6
1948	63.4	36.6	44.3	55.7	22.3	77.7
1949	61.2	38.8	57	43	41.7	58.3
1950	64.2	35.8	46.8	53.2	31	69
1951	61.4	38.6	35.8	64.2	20.6	79.4
1952	71.2	28.8	65.7	34.3	36.8	63.2
1953	74.8	25.2	12.2	87.8	18	82
1954 (Jan.-April)	73	27	56.4	43.6	41.5	58.5

to strike remains very high[1]. Table III above, to which we have already made references, shows (i) the number of stoppages, (ii) workers involved, and (iii) days lost in coal-mining as a percentage of (i), (ii) and (iii) in all industries in the United Kingdom during the period 1946–1954. The high incidence of disputes in mining is not peculiar to United Kingdom alone. Writing about Australia, E. R. Walker says: "Of all Australian industries coal has given by far the most trouble in the form of production lost through apparently avoidable causes, including industrial stoppages and absenteeism"[2].

It is difficult to classify in any rigid way the causes which give rise to stoppages and restrictions in coal-mining. The following "causes" selected at random from the Coal Board's weekly returns are reproduced below to show that a number of disputes are caused everyday by the most varied and, sometimes, trifling factors:

---

[1] Prof. Knowles places the "industrial strike-proneness ratio" in mining and quarrying (*i.e.*, percentage of strikers ÷ percentage of industrial population) for the period January 1911 — June 1945 at 6.7; for textiles, 4.3; for metal, engineering and shipbuilding, 1.3; for transport, 1.1; for building, 0.4; for clothing, 0.4; for other industries and services, 0.1.
(Paper at International Sociological Association, *op. cit.*, Table VI).

[2] *The Australian Economy in War and Reconstruction*, New York, Oxford University Press, 1947, p. 311.

1) The Manager complained of short notice being given for Branch Committee meeting. N.U.M. officials objected to Manager's attitude and left meeting. Men stopped work in protest.
2) Packers dissatisfied with wages. Resumed pre-stoppage conditions.
3) Men adopted a "go-slow" policy due to Manager stopping allowance for disturbed conditions. Management allege conditions have returned to normal.
4) Men returned home not satisfied with progress made with mechanisation.
5) Men returned home refusing to descend owing to spake having become derailed. They alleged that it was not safe to ride but Management stated that it was.
6) 26 boys returned home after asking Manager for permisson to leave early to attend funeral of a boy who had worked with them. Management refused but was prepared to grant permission to 3 boys but they rejected the offer.
7) Men found taking a spell at 8.50 a.m. They were sent out by Management.
8) A drawer was refused permission to go down pit as he had been leaving early for a few days. The rest of the men came out in sympathy.
9) Man dismissed for smoking underground. Others came out in sympathy.

The following table, based on information collected from the Coal Board's Office, gives the approximate figures of the number of disputes, tonnage lost (raised and weighed) and percentage of loss classified according to causes for the period 1947–1952.

TABLE IV

Details of Causes	Total for six years, i.e., 1947–1952		
	No. of Disputes	Tonnage lost	Percentage of total loss
(a) Disputes regarding allowances and bonuses	556	379,288	4.6
(b) Refusal to accept reasonable alternative work	722	184,895	2.2
(c) Sympathy with men dismissed, suspended or reprimanded	245	177,289	2.1
(d) Refusal to perform work left from previous shift	317	73,983	0.9
(e) Disputes regarding terms and conditions of Five-Day Week Agreement	86	853,561	10.3
(f) Refusal to await repairs after mechanical breakdown	275	66,552	0.8
(g) Objection to or disputes regarding officials.	80	85,580	1.0
(h) Personnel and Grading questions.	291	101,131	1.2
(i) Disputes regarding wages and price lists	4,472	4,475,140	54.0
(j) Alleged bad working conditions .	1,075	310,689	3.7
(k) Disagreement regarding methods of working and general organisation	1,592	905,634	10.9
(l) Miscellaneous (including disputes regarding fatal accidents, agreements, perquisites, loss of tools, letting N.C.B. houses etc.). . . .	593	308,866	3.7
(m) Concessionary Coal dispute (1949)	108	382,590	4.6
Total	10,412	8,305,198	100

Note:
(i) Tonnages lost are estimations based on "Raised and Weighed tonnages";
(ii) Figures take into account all stoppages and restrictions however small;
(iii) Figures also include stoppages and restrictions of work at Ancillary undertakings and licensed mines;
(iv) Stoppages and restrictions which occur at one or more collieries in connection with the same dispute are recorded in the "number of disputes" as separate incidents;
(v) Stoppages and restrictions in progress at 31st December 1952 are included in the figures.

Wages and disputes: From Table IV we find that more than half of the total loss from disputes arose from questions concerning "wages and price-lists". In order to bring home to the reader the great diversity and complexity of the present wages structure in the industry, it would be essential to outline very briefly how the present system of wages has evolved through the course of years. In the main, the present system of paying the miners derives from the wages settlement made in 1921. The miner's wage was divided into (i) a basis wage, and (ii) a percentage addition to the basis wage. The basis wage referred to the piece-work rate for face and contract workers, and to a day-wage for other workers, both underground and surface. It differed from district to district. The percentage addition was settled on the "ascertainment" system. The total proceeds less all costs other than wages were calculated, and the remaining amount was apportioned between wages and profits in a fixed proportion. The proportion varied from district to district. Instead of promoting industrial peace, which the "ascertainment"system was expected to do, it created increased industrial unrest.

The advent of the Second World War brought an increase in industrial costs, except wages, and the disposable proceeds showed a tendency to fall[1]. On 20th March, 1940, an agreement was reached known as the War Additions to Wages Agreement. The important features of the Agreement were as follows: it provided for the continuance, during the war-period, of the district wage arrangements, subject to mutually agreed alterations. Necessary account was to be taken of exceptional conditions, especially the increase in the cost-of-living, in which case uniform flat rate additions were to be granted on a national basis. As from the 1st January until 31st March 1940, the flat rate additions were paid at the rate of 1s. 1d. per shift for adult workers, and 6½d. per shift for others. The rates to be paid from 1st April, 1940 were to be determined as follows: the cost-of-living index published by the Ministry of Labour was to be reviewed quarterly to ascertain the rise, if any, above the figure of 155, the figure at which the index stood immediately before the outbreak of the war. For the next three months, the War Addition to adult workers' wages was to be calculated by multiplying 0.7 d.to the number of points recorded above the 155 mark. Workers other than adults were to be paid at one half of the rate paid to adults. "Adult" was to be interpreted according to the custom of each district. The agreement could be terminated by any party giving a notice of six months, which could be done only after, not before, the cessation of hostilities[2].

---

[1] W. H. B. Court, *op. cit.*, p. 221.

[2] For a full text of the Agreement, see N.C.B. *Memorandum of Agreements, etc.*, Part I, Period 20th March, 1940 to 31st July, 1946, pp. 8–9.

A second important change during World War II came when the Greene Committee of 1942 suggested that the principle of a national minimum wage for the industry should be adopted. It declared: "We consider that the principle of a national minimum wage for the industry ought to be accepted"[1]. It recommended the "adoption of an overriding minimum wage of 83s. a week for all adult underground workers and a miminum wage of 78s. for all adult surface workers"[2]. Besides the fixation of the minimum wage, the Board also outlined a scheme for the payment of an "Output Bonus". The urgent necessity for increasing the production of coal during the war time weighed with the Committee to work out the plan for Output Bonus. The object of the scheme was "to give additional remuneration to the workers whenever the monthly output of saleable coal in their district exceeds the standard output for the district by at least one percent"[3]. Standard outputs were decided for different districts and a graduated scale of payment of bonus was laid down.

By its fourth "Porter" Award in January 1944, the National Reference Tribunal increased the minimum wage to 100s. a week for adult underground workers and 90s. in the case of those employed on the surface[4]. The one important effect of this Award was that it disturbed the wage differentials which had existed in the industry. Miners whose rates differed previously now found themselves getting the same wages. The disappearance of the wage differentials created confusion and bred discontent among the miners, a trouble which the Tribunal had wanted to avoid[5]. By lessening the proportion of the pieceworker's wage which he could earn by his extra effort, the flat-rate additions reduced the incentives for increasing production. It also reduced the ratio of the earnings of piece-workers *vis-a-vis* the daywage-men and became a potential source of heart-burning amongst the former upon whom the industry depended so much for the increase in output. The "Porter" Award had also recommended

[1] *Report of the Board of Investigation into the Immediate Wage Issue in the Coal-mining Industry*, para. 9.
[2] *ibid.*, para. 10.
[3] Coal-Mining Industry — Output Bonus, *Supplemental Report by the Board of Investigation*, para. 1.
[4] See, the Fourth "Porter" Award in the N.C.B. *Memorandum of Agreements, etc.*, Part I, 20th March, 1940 to 31st July, 1946, p. 56.
[5] For a fuller discussion, see, W. H. B. Court, *op. cit.*, p. 253 ff.

a thorough overhaul of the wages-structure which, the Tribunal thought, was long overdue. Later on, in order to counteract the dulling effect of flat-rate additions on the incentives for increasing production, all existing flat-rates, except the war-time cost-of-living bonus, were merged into the piece-work rates. This was done by an Agreement signed on 20th April 1944 between the Mineworkers' Federation and the Mining Association. It also put an end to the "ascertainment" system[1].

The idea in tracing briefly the evolution of the wages-structure in the industry has been to show that what the National Coal Board inherited was not a simple, clearly designed system of wage-payments. On the contrary, it was a highly intricate and diverse system which differed from district to district. Besides, all over the country, the miners are entitled to various perquisites and allowances, which, again, are unequal in different coalfields. Though the trends towards uniformity in the wages-structure were discernible before the advent of nationalisation, they have not yet culminated into a definite systematized method of wage-payment over the country as a whole[2]. Where piecework rates apply, they are negotiated between the workers and the Board. Geological conditions, the difficulty of cutting coal from thinner seams and the bargaining skills of the two parties all play their part in the drawing up of price-lists. It is small wonder, therefore, that numerous disputes arise everyday on questions of wages.

The hang-over from past relationships. Any attempt which tries to explain the reason for the frequency of disputes in coal-mining today without referring to the past history of industrial relations in the industry will be incomplete. Writing under the subtitle of "Grievances of the Miners", the *Royal Commission on the Coal Industry* (1925) says:

> Account must be taken of the fact, in the first place, that the present grievances of the mining population are frequently viewed by them in association with the grievances

[1] Clause 2 (i) of the Agreement says: "The existing ascertainment agreements shall be suspended for the duration of this agreement, such percentage additions as are at present payable thereunder being merged in the day-wages or piece-rates payable as provided herein".

[2] In this connection, see our discussion of the Concessionary Coal Dispute of 1949 and the Wage-dispute of 1952, Chapter V.

> of the past. They are well aware of the history of their industry. Through reading and through family tradition, abuses which have been remedied and which may be forgotten by others are kept alive in the memory[1].

The Commission wrote this in 1925, but this fact remains true even now, though in many parts an increasing contact with the outside world is responsible for a gradual loosening of the hold of old customs and traditions. Possibly, the comparatively isolated nature of the Scottish and Welsh coalfields is one of the reasons for the higher frequency of disputes in those regions[2]. The history of the worker-employer relations in the coal industry has been very unhappy. In an urban industry the unpleasant memories would have slipped into oblivion, but in mining they continue to live afresh and exercise a profound influence on the attitude of the miners. It is quite common to find a miner mentally re-live the past while evaluating the worth of a new reform. By drawing parallels from the past, a new measure initiated by the Coal Board may be seen in an entirely different light. Increasing mechanisation may thus come to be looked upon as a threat of unemployment and, therefore, a justifiable excuse for strike. As the Reid Report pointed out, the miners though seldom actively opposing the introduction of machinery, never received it with enthusiasm. Even where mechanisation was introduced, its beneficial effects were wiped out by a determination to keep the number of workers displaced to the lowest possible extent. The sociological structure of many mining communities makes the perpetuation of these ideas possible, and also provides a natural ground for the formation of a democratic Trade Union machine.[3] Historically speaking, there had always been a short working week in the industry. The wages were generally low and wherever work was available, it was not available for the full week[4]. The conception of short working

---

[1] Volume I, Report, Cmd. 2600, 1926, p. 108.

[2] "A community", writes Elton Mayo "which has been accustomed to a certain manner of living offers resistance to change in proportion as it has held its integrate character".
The Human Problems of an Industrial Civilization, Graduate School of Business Administration, Harvard University, 1946, pp. 131–132.

[3] Cole, *Labour in the Coal-Mining Industry*, *op. cit.*, 1923, p. 7.

[4] In the 1927 Report of the Executive Committee of the Miners' Federation of Great Britain, under the title "The Economic Position of the Industry,

week, therefore, still dominates the attitude of the miners and when the pits are now open all through the week, it becomes one of the reasons for the high rate of absenteeism which the industry records. According to one source, while in the past absenteeism was caused by the lack of work and by the custom of the miners working for some part of the year in agriculture, "with the present demand for output and shortage of workers, it is nearly always on the miner's initiative"[1].

Dangerous nature of the work. The dangerous and difficult type of work underground is another factor which contributes to the frequency of disputes. Thus:

> Miners are not averse to striking on slight pretext. They like to "play" at intervals, and then, return to scrabble harder in the pits, whence they can direct their thoughts with some contempt to the people who have to pass all their hours on the surface[2].

Sometimes difficult conditions of working coal from thinner seams or some geological fault or the existence of water-hazard creates complications in the adjustment of wages which are to be paid for working in abnormal conditions and lead to disputes.

Technical reorganisation and disputes. The need for technical improvements in the industry is great, and any scheme which seeks to increase productivity will have to contend itself with the gigantic task of replacing the obsolete methods of mining by modern ones. "In its infancy and youth", said Mr. E. H. Browne, "the mining of coal was a kind of natural art or a craft; but today it is an industrial engineering complex, technically as elaborate as any, and one of the most exacting ones in the world

---

and the Policy of the Federation in Relation Thereto", we come across the following: "The fundamental trouble of the industry is the same in every coal-producing country of the world; it can be stated in five words: "EXCESS OF SUPPLY OVER DEMAND".

The causes of this trouble, which the Report described as "natural causes of a permanent nature", were: (i) Increased use of coal substitutes and the increasing efficacy of methods of coal conservation; and (ii) Expansion of coal production in other countries and their desire to make themselves independent of foreign coal supplies.

[1] Scott and Lynton, *Three Studies in Management*, Routledge and Kegan Paul, London, 1952, p. 30.

[2] Lord Askwith, *op. cit.*, p. 201.

to manage"[1]. The urgent need for raising the productivity in the industry would mean introducing more mechanical methods of cutting, loading and carrying coal to the roadways. We do not advocate indiscriminate mechanization, however. Conditions differ from pit to pit, and where coal lies near the surface, mechanization may not prove to be economical. The point we would like to emphasize here is that greater use of mechanized methods of coal-getting, involving change in work-patterns, will have a profound influence on the course of conflict in the industry. It has been shown that the replacement of the hand-got system by the longwall method of obtaining coal brought about a totally different set of work-relationships[2]. Workers may experience increased stresses if the introduction of machinery involves on the part of the individual a complex adjustment of intellect, emotions, habits and body, and this difficult process might manifest itself in a larger number of disputes.

Disputes and the conciliation machinery

In our discussion of the course of conflict in the coal-mining industry in the earlier parts of this chapter, there are occasional references to the use which was made of the conciliation machinery in case of disputes.

The following table, based on figures collected from the office of the National Coal Board, presents an analysis of the percentage of stoppages and restrictions in the industry in relation to the conciliation machinery for the period 1949–1953.

---

[1] *The Cadman Memorial Lecture*, Improving Coal Production, (Mimeographed), p. 7, (obtainable from the N.C.B.)

[2] See:

(i) E. L. Trist and K. W. Bamforth, Social and Psychological Consequences of the Longwall Method of Coal-getting, *Human Relations*, Vol. IV, No. 1, February 1951. Writing about the change from the Hand-got to the Longwall Method of coal-getting, the authors point out: "The associated characteristics of mechanized complexity, and of largeness as regards the scale of the primary production unit, created a situation in which it was impossible for the method to develop as a technological system without bringing into existence a work relationship structure radically different from that associated with hand-got procedures".

(ii) A. T. M. Wilson, Some Aspects of Social Process, *Journal of Social Issues*, No. 5, 1951.

(iii) Einar Thorsrud, The Social Consequences of Technical Change from the Psychological Standpoint, *U.N.E.S.C.O. International Social Science Bulletin*, Vol. IV, No. 2, Summer 1952, pp. 305–306.

TABLE V

Year	Stage of conciliation reached prior to stoppage or restriction											
	Nil	1	2	3	4	5	6	7	8	9	10	11
1949	4.8	39.9	32.3	6.8	1.0	1.5	0.6			7.1	6.0	
1950	11.6	42.1	31.9	6.9	1.0	1.0	1.0	0.05	0.05	2.1		2.3
1951	2.7	39.4	41.8	8.7	2.6	3.0	1.0	0.7		0.1		
1952	6.4	28.6	39.8	5.1	2.1	0.4	0.4	2.2		1.1	11.1	2.9
1953	8.6	42.5	33.1	6.7	3.1	0.6	0.1				5.3	

Stages for 1949, 1950 and 1951

1. Discussions between men and pit official.
2. Discussions between men and manager
3. Discussions between manager and union official.
4. Dispute discussed at pit meeting.
5. Dispute discussed at disputes committee.
6. Dispute referred to Umpire.
7. Dispute referred to District Conciliation Board as District Question
8. Dispute referred to Referee.
9. Dispute discussed at Nat. Conciliation Board.
10. Informal talks nationally.
11. Dispute referred to Nat. Reference Tribunal.

Stages for 1952 and 1953

1.–8. Same

9. Dispute discussed at Nat. Negotiating Committee.
10. Dispute referred to Nat. Reference Tribunal.
11. Informal talks Divisionally or Nationally.

It must be said, however, that the table presents the picture of the entire industry and conceals the regional differences which can be substantial. However, in an over-all estimate it can be pointed out that a large percentage of the disputes just touch the conciliation machinery, but this contact is not sustained and tends to break off after discussions between men and manager have taken place. A factor which contributes to this situation is the delay involved in settling a dispute by submitting it to the conciliation machinery. Thus, according to one source: "Delays in getting grievances settled were a common catalyst of strikes. Sometimes a strike settlement would be negotiated only to be followed by another strike against delays in these negotiations"[1].

The Frequency of Small Disputes

In Table VI below we have classified the disputes according to those which caused a loss in output of (i) less than 10,000 tons, (ii) over 10,000 tons but less than 100,000 tons, and (iii) 100,000 tons and over. The number of disputes are shown under each classification and the amount of loss arising therefrom is presented as a percentage of the total annual loss. The Table covers the period 1947–1953.

[1] W. W. Haynes, *Nationalization in Practice: The British Coal Industry*, Bailey Bros. & Swinfen Ltd., 1953, p. 167.

TABLE VI

Year	Disputes which caused a loss of less than 10,000 tons		Disputes which caused a loss of 10,000 tons and over but less than 100,000 tons		Disputes which caused a loss of 100,000 tons and over	
	No. of disputes	Loss shown as % of Total loss (Approx.)	No. of disputes	Loss shown as % of Total loss (Approx.)	No. of disputes	Loss shown as % of Total loss (Approx.)
1947	1,628	42	5	14	2	44[1]
1948	1,519	71	7	10	2	19
1949	1,626	39	6	15	2	46[2]
1950	1,604	60	8	18	1	22
1951	1,624	74	12	16	1	10
1952	2,351	54	17	26	2	20
1953	2,315	86	9	14	—	—

Notes:

(i) In calculating the percentage of loss, the "raised and weighed" output has been taken into account.
(ii) Disputes caused by the same factor in different Divisions, *e.g.*, stoppages consequent on the 24th "Porter" Award, have been counted separately.
(iii) Both stoppages and "go-slows" have been included.
(iv) Disputes could also be classified according to (i) the number of workers affected, and (ii) aggregate duration of working-days lost. The non-availability of statistics precludes us from adopting any of these two classifications.

[1] This includes the loss arising out of the Grimethorpe strike.
[2] The year 1949 recorded the Winding Enginemen's and the Concessionary Coal Claim Disputes.

From the above Table it is clear that an overwhelming majority of the disputes are small and cause a loss of less than 10,000 tons. It would be difficult to make any generalisations about these numerous small disputes. With the exception of the years 1947 and 1949, the greater percentage of loss was caused by small disputes. The number of disputes, which caused a loss in output of 100,000 tons and over, never exceeded two in one year, though the percentage of loss from disputes in this category was, with the exception of 1951 and 1953, substantial. In short, the tendency for disputes to assume large dimensions seems to be on the decline.

Summary

While the coal-mining industry is now marked by the absence of long drawn-out strikes, a large number of small disputes cause a vital portion of the loss every year. Generalisations about these disputes are not easy to make. The propensity of the miners to strike remains high, though this is nothing exceptional to Britain. It is difficult to ascertain with any precision the causes of the numerous small disputes, which take place in the industry. In the majority of cases, however, the overt cause is the wage-issue. The present wages structure, which is the result of a long process of evolution, carries the traces of local variations. In addition to wages, working conditions, provision of alternative work, sympathy with men dismissed or suspended, performance of work left from previous shift, technical reorganisation and some other factors cause disputes. The situation is aggravated by the history of past bad industrial relations which lives vividly in the memories of the miners. Generally speaking, the conciliation machinery is not utilized fully before a dispute deteriorates into a stoppage or a restriction of work.

CHAPTER IV

UNOFFICIAL STRIKES

An important feature of the strikes, which needs some consideration, is their "unofficial" nature, i.e., the strikers are not entitled to receive strike-pay from the funds of the union. The large frequency of such disputes and the changed role of the trade unions have, however, given a loose meaning to the term "unofficial" strikes.

Before we examine the *raison d'être* of "unofficial" strikes in coal-mining, it would be relevant to present the broader historical and organisational factors which have shaped a situation wherein such strikes have become almost inevitable and, what is more, occasionally act as a healthy check against the tendencies towards centralization. These trends are discernible in the trade unions today.

Historical Factors

To understand the psychology of the workers' organisations, we have to take into consideration the hostile environment in which they have developed. Looking back in retrospect now from the middle of the 20th century, it is easy enough to condemn the extreme and repressive measures taken by the employers and the governments against the trade unions in the 19th and early 20th centuries. It is equally easy to show surprise as to why the workers were denied the right to unite and to express their opinions freely on matters which concerned them directly. But viewed against the background of the dominant economic philosophy of those times, the position becomes easy to understand. The rising class of industrialists, guided by the philosophy of *laissez-faire* and aided by mechanical inventions, had brought into existence huge factories, whose products satisfied the needs of ever expanding markets and made possible vast aggregations of wealth. On this rapidly expanding economic structure, the trade unions appeared as fetters and looked like trespassing on a domain which the *entrepreneur* considered to be his very own. Oftentimes, trade unions were considered to be in "restraint of trade"[1]. It would be irrelevant for our purposes to trace in any details the difficulties and hardships which the trade unions had to face in different countries. Any history of the trade union movement will bear ample testimony to our statement[2]. Suffice it to say that the employers and the governments alike tried to counter the growth of unions by methods of victimisation of the active members, formation of "scab-unions", enacting anti-workers' legislation, etc. But even today when the unions have come to stay as institutions representing the workers' interests in society, hostility towards them has not completely disappeared. Nor has their role of opposition ceased. The growth of the systems of joint consultation and collective bargaining has not entirely removed the risks to which the workers are exposed in modern society. Despite the vast array of figures of membership, finances etc., through which some trade union journals seek to exhibit the unions' strength, the role of the unions remains basically defensive. Within the narrow range of the industry, the worker remains the tool to carry out the employers' wishes, though it must be pointed out that in highly unionized industries the employers' scope for exercising arbitrary judgment has been strictly restricted. But the wider swings of the business cycles, against which the individual employer is helpless, lay bare the workers to the risks of reductions in wages and unemployment.

To the average worker, then, the trade union functions as a body which safeguards his interests and is ready to take up the cudgels when the worst threatens. The effect of this has been to

---

[1] For a legal treatment see, N. A. Citrine, *Trade Union Law*, Chapter 2, Stevens and Sons Limited, London, 1950. "The doctrine of restraint of trade is not one which is special to trade unions, although the nature of their objects renders their rules and agreements specially susceptible to its influence". (p. 28).

Also, Webbs, *History of Trade Unionism*, 1950 impression, p. 611 ff.

[2] The Webbs wrote: "It is a characteristic feature of Trade Union history, at the end as at the beginning of the record of the past hundred years, that we have to trace the advance of the Movement through a series of attacks upon Trade Unionism itself". *ibid.*, p. 594.

develop in the trade unions a psychology to oppose. As Prof. Cole says: "It (Trade Unionism) bears the stigmata of its history upon it: its members have never expected to be fairly treated, and, when the unexpected happens, can hardly recognise it for what it is"[1]. The "unofficial" strike in this sense reflects the strain which is inevitably experienced by the rank-and-file of the workers in adjusting to the changed functions of trade unions in modern society. So long as the avowed aim of the trade unions was to fight their way for getting more and more wages for their members, frequent strikes provided both an outlet for the workers' grievances and also an affirmation of their confidence in the leaders. The leaders gave the call and the rank-and-file obeyed. But when the trade unions came to be accepted as an integral part of the industrial structure, and when their leaders began to sit with the employers for discussing problems of mutual interest, the rift between the leaders and the rank-and-file began to show itself. By a strange paradox, once the very aim for which the unions had battled relentlessly was achieved, the leaders found themselves in a predicament. An agreement which results from the joint discussions between the representatives of the employers and the workers places a responsibility on the shoulders of the union leaders. The employer has as much right to expect the leaders and, through them, the rank-and-file of the workers to honour the agreement as the Union has to ask the employer to abide by the terms and conditions of the agreement. The union leader has now to turn around and convince the rank-and-file into adhering strictly to the clauses of the agreement[2]. Can he do it?[3]

Centralisation in Trade Unions

An answer to the above question will necessarily take us into an examination of the internal organisation of the trade unions and into an analysis of the position of the leader in relation to the rank-and-file of the workers. A fact which has an important

---

[1] G. D. H. Cole, *An Introduction to Trade Unionism*, George Allen & Unwin Ltd., 1953, Chapter X, p. 207.

[2] This is not to say that the opinions of the rank-and-file are not at all reflected in the agreements.

[3] See the interesting discussion in, Peter F. Drucker, *op. cit.*, Chapter 13, "The Union Leader's Dilemma", pp. 129–145.

bearing on the amount of obedience which the leader can command from the workers is the growing size of the trade unions. Through a process of amalgamation the trade unions of to-day have become massive organisations, with their membership scattered in all parts of the country. In Britain the last two decades of the 19th century witnessed a general tendency towards centralization in trade union organisation. Sidney Webb wrote in 1921: "During the past decade the British Trade Union Movement has been stirred by a powerful impulse to amalgamation among the several societies"[1]. The reason for the formation of these aggregations was "to strengthen the power of the combined workers, not merely to increase wages and to shorten the hours of labour, but to acquire an increasing share in the positive management of the industry by which they live"[2]. The growth of industrial unions, which cut across the narrow frontiers of crafts, brought about a tendency towards the centralisation of the union affairs. This also led to a change in the administrative set-up of the trade unions. Methods of primitive democracy which could function well in small organisations became hopelessly inadequate for big organisations, and meticulously prepared ballot papers and voting procedures began to lay the foundations of modern trade union government. This led to the emergence of a trade union bureaucracy manned by full-time officials. The hierarchical structure thus formed almost inevitably created a gulf between the leaders and the rank-and-file. This is not to say that the leader is imposed from above; generally he "rises from the ranks", but by the time he reaches the top he becomes a distant person to those whom he has left behind. The contact between him and his followers, despite the existence of constitutional checks, becomes slender. Undoubtedly, many leaders continue to keep in touch with the rest of the workers through effective channels of communication and other devices. But there remains a genuine danger of a situation arising where the leader may find it difficult to ask his followers to abide by a decision which he has arrived at after joint consultations with the employers.

[1] *International Labour Review*, Vol. I, No. 1, January 1921, "Amalgamation in British Trade Unionism", p. 47.
[2] *ibid.*, p. 57.

The Leader and the Rank-and-File

One of the factors which adds to the widening gap between the leader and the mass of the workers lies in the very nature of the duties which the former is called upon to discharge. His functions are of a much more specialized nature than the average worker can understand. It is true that a large part of the discussions between the unions and the employers converges on the day to day problems which face the workers, such as questions of wages, hours of work, working conditions, etc. But sitting at the apex of the organisation, the leader views the problems from a higher angle and surveys a wider scene than confronts the average worker. He begins to concern himself with problems of costs and productivity, which to the majority of workers sound as theoretical jargons. An increase in wages, the leader may be convinced, will have inflationary consequences and, if the industry is of a basic nature, give a blow to the nation's economy. From a position where an increase in the wages of the workers is considered to be the supreme goal, he now gets involved in technical problems which the integrated nature of modern economies necessarily raises. The leader appreciates all this and, with the best of intentions, asks his followers to forego a demand which would only apparently, and not actually, benefit them. The leaders' position has been excellently summed up by Prof. Hoxie in the following words:

> Responsibility sobers them. As soon as they engage in negotiations they realize the power of the employers, and the limitations in the ability of employers to meet demands. Moreover, when the leaders get away from the bench, their environment becomes more of the character of the employer's than of the worker's. They no longer deal with the physical, but with the spiritual, in negotiations and in the handling of men. Almost inevitably they develop something of the employer's viewpoint and feeling, and thus become unable to see things from the workers' angle and to feel with and for the workers as before[1].

The workers, if properly approached, may appreciate the leader's viewpoint. But on occasions they may not understand the language of the leader and may rebel, thus causing "un-

[1] R. F. Hoxie, *Trade Unionism in the United States*, D. Appleton & Co., 1917, pp. 179–180.

official" strikes. It would not be correct to condemn the workers outright. By the very environment in which they are placed, they are concerned more with the immediate than with the ultimate. Their wages, working arrangements, the behaviour of the foremen, their own position in the primary work-group and such other day-to-day factors condition their views on their relationship with the employer and on the role which, they think, their union ought to play.

Sometimes the acquisition of power and prestige may have an unsteadying influence on the leader and make him oblivious of the role which he, as the guardian of the workers' interests, has to play. To quote once again from Hoxie:

> Many go wrong because they cannot stand prosperity. The sudden release from the bench, from the machine process, unsteadies them; they become dissipated and dishonest; they may fall victims to the "mahogany table", and to what is on it. There is, too, a constant drain of leaders by corruption, and by politics. Here is a great weakness of unionism — it dies at the top[1].

The Nature of the Leader's Duties

The above might appear to be a harsh verdict on the leaders. Lest our remarks be exaggerated, we may now set out briefly the nature of the leader's tasks. These are by no means easy and, for successful execution, call for the combination of qualities which range from keeping a cool head in the face of scathing criticisms from the union's own ranks, to the adoption of subtle manoeuvres of the cleverest nature while dealing with the employers. In his capacity of the head of a big trade union organisation, the leader has not only to further the aims of the members, but also to steer a course which may not jeopardise the interests of the community at large. It is the reconciliation of these two interests, which may — and generally do — diverge, which provides the most difficult task of the leader[2]. It is he who, in the face of the rejection of a claim by the employers when feelings are highly

[1] *ibid.*, p. 180. It may be pointed out here that Prof. Hoxie had the American labour movement of his days in mind. In the present context, this would be an overstatement.

[2] V. L. Allen, *Power in Trade Unions*, Longmans Green & Co., 1954. "He cannot be fair in his dealings unless he disciplines himself: he must be able to examine workers' demands and complaints objectively and realistically

explosive, has to ask his followers to take the rough with the smooth. In short, as one writer puts it: "The requirements for successful union leadership will become increasingly higher and increasingly harder to meet. Both the labor movement and society need a union leadership of exceptional intellectual ability, of exceptional emotional maturity, of exceptional experience, and of exceptional integrity"[1].

For the discharge of his duties and for attaining the Union's objectives, the leader considers it essential to inculcate certain attitudes in the rank-and-file of the workers. However, it is not always the leader who is the source of attitudes. Union experiences, particularly during times of crisis, leave impressions on the minds of the workers which may last for a long time. How far the leader succeeds in achieving the above-mentioned objective will differ with different leaders and unions[2]. If he is clever and, despite his top position, maintains close and continuous contact with the mass of the workers, he may succeed; if not, there remains the possibility that workers would turn upon him and wreck him. The possibility that the leader or the national officials would be dislodged by the rank-and-file remains, generally speaking, only a theoretical proposition. No doubt, the constitutions of trade unions provide for the dismissal of the leader[3]. Even the "vivid and direct" pressures exercised by members of the union on the leader, in the shape of a constant clamour for higher wages, provide a continuous challenge to the latter[4]. Notwithstanding all this, the leader once elected to the office has certain advantages which make his expulsion a difficult affair.

before he presents them to the employers, and he must be able to appraise them against a background of wider issues of national trade-union policy and national economic policy; to project himself from the particular to the general".

Part II, Chapter III, p. 197. Entitled "Trade-Union Leaders", the chapter provides an excellent discussion of the British scene.

[1] *The Annals of the American Academy of Political and Social Science*, March 1951, article by Peter F. Drucker, "Labor in Industrial Society", p. 149.

[2] For a case study on this aspect, see A. M. Rose, *Union Solidarity*, The University of Minnesota Press, 1952, Chapter IV, "The Extent to Which Members Agree with Union Policies".

[3] A comparative analysis of the principal sources of constitutional power in 127 British Trade Unions can be found in, Allen, *op. cit.*, Table 1, pp. 74–99.

[4] B. M. Selekman, *Labor Relations and Human Relations*, McGraw-Hill Book Co., 1947, Chapter VIII, p. 177.

The Sources of the Leader's Power

We have already drawn attention to the growth of centralisation in trade unions. The centralised nature of administration has deposited considerable powers in the hands of the national leaders. To a certain extent, by shifting away the duties which were formerly the concern of the people at the local level to the national plane, the leaders have made themselves indispensable to the unions. This, incidentally, is also one of the factors which explains the apathy of the average members in a big workers' organisation[1]. Once the leader occupies the position where he represents the workers before the employers, he becomes the central figure and the rank-and-file of workers begin to lean heavily on his dexterity for presenting their case before the management. The average worker knows that he himself is no match against the bargaining skill of the employer who is generally aided by a staff of professional experts. The longer the leader stays in office, the more acquainted he becomes with the problems involved in worker-management relationship. Experience ripens him into a master strategist, an able administrator and an efficient organizer. The local member reads about his achievements on the distant national scene in the newspapers and derives an emotional satisfaction from the fact that both of them belong to the same organisation. All this, needless to say, helps to install the leader more firmly in his position. Thus, in a way, the leader perpetuates his position[2].

A second factor, which makes the emergence of organized opposition difficult, is inherent in the nature of trade union organisation. A trade union, unlike the community at large, is essentially a single-purpose organisation. Though sometimes in large industrial unions the interests of different sections of workers may vary and give rise to internal cleavages, these differences are likely to be submerged within the wider uniformity of the purposes of a union. A trade union is an organisation which seeks to advance the interests of its members and any opposition is, therefore, looked upon as breaking the unity of the union. Opposition within a trade union is, therefore, discouraged, and

[1] For a case study, see, Joseph Goldstein, *The Government of British Trade Unions*, Allen & Unwin Ltd., 1952, especially Parts II and III.

[2] See, Hoxie, *op. cit.*, pp. 182–185.

unless there is a powerful alternative leadership with a substantial following, it is very likely that the leader will continue in his position till he retires. The broader uniformity of interests is emphasized by the basically defensive role which the trade unions play in modern society and to which we have already drawn attention. Constant fights with the employers, though their duration and intensity have now considerably declined, act as a cohesive force which tends to draw the workers closer together. Viewed from this standpoint, the trade union can be seen as an aggregation of like-minded individuals. The administrative staff, the constitution and the conferences of the unions provide only the external manifestation of the mutuality of interests of members, while the more effective bond is "a consciousness of common needs and aims, a common outlook on life, and a common program for the betterment of their lot"[1].

Sometimes the union constitutions prohibit the circulation of literature which is critical of national leadership or the setting up of organized oppositions and thus subdue the emergence of rival leadership. Even where such an activity is permitted, "formal and organised oppositions, founded on a trade union rather than on an ideological basis, seem to vanish with time"[2].

It goes without saying that the above remarks are not meant to be of universal applicability. Instances can be found where the union members have been able to dislodge the leader through constitutional means, but these are in the nature of exceptions and do not affect the general validity of our argument.

This rather lengthy excursion into the position of the leader in relation to the rank-and-file has been necessitated by our conviction that no explanation of the numerous "unofficial" strikes which take place everyday in industries, would be comprehensive enough unless into it takes account the problems we have analysed above.

These, then, are the two important facts; first, that the trade unions developed in an environment where they had to oppose incessantly the onslaughts of the employers and of the governments of the day; and, secondly, that the present organisational

[1] Introduction to Hoxie, *op. cit.*, p. xvi by E. H. Downey.
[2] *Annals*, *op. cit.*, article by Philip Taft, "Internal Characteristics of American Unionism", p. 99.

set-up of the trade unions is tending to create a gulf between the national leadership and the rank-and-file of the members. The impact of these two factors on the origin of "unofficial" strikes is clear and direct.

"Unofficial" Strikes in Coal-Mining

Having set out the broader forces which are at work in the labour organisations and their impact on the origin of "unofficial" strikes, we shall now focus our attention on the coal industry.

This calls for an examination of the organisational set-up of the N.U.M. The N.U.M. assumed its present centralized shape after a resolution providing for the formation of a single national union was adopted at the Nottingham Conference of 1944[1]. The present centralized structure has brought about a change in the relative positions of the local lodges and the districts in relation to the central executive of the Union. This change can be understood if we examine it in its historical perspective and try to show how over the course of years the seat of power has been gradually shifting from the districts to the centre.

The Movement Towards Centralization in the N.U.M.[2]

Originally, the miners' unions were district organisations which grew up locally in response to the needs of particular areas. The widespread distribution of the mines over the whole country had brought into existence miners' organisations which were very active on the district level but which, despite the existence of M.F.G.B., had not been formed into a powerful national organisation. The important point to be kept in mind is the almost complete autonomy which each district union enjoyed. The independent handling of the problems by each district in its own way, without interference from the national organisation, had brought into vogue practices which were very different in different parts of the country. As we shall try to show in the next

[1] After the Nottingham Conference, the Mineworkers' Federation of Great Britain was re-named the National Union of Mineworkers.

[2] In the discussion which follows, we have benefitted from the article: "Structural Reform in the British Miners' Union" by George B. Baldwin in the *Quarterly Journal of Economics*, Vol. LXVII, No. 4, November 1953, pp. 576–597.

chapter, this lack of uniformity in the different districts appears to be one of the thorniest problems which the Coal Board has now to contend with. The independence enjoyed by the district organisations obstructed the emergence of a central and effective leadership which could speak on behalf of the workers employed in the mining industry on a national basis. The central office in London maintained a skeleton staff, and unless specifically invited by the district union, it could not even send its representatives to inquire into the affairs of the districts.

The Federation, however, represented the miners on the Trade Union Congress. It also provided a platform where industry-wide problems could be discussed. But it had no authority to force any district union to submit to a centrally evolved policy.

The severe strikes of 1921 and 1926 had resulted in the complete defeat of the miners' organisation. Some of the biggest district unions found their funds considerably depleted, and the mass unemployment of the depression period worsened the already hopeless condition in which the district unions found themselves. Amongst the miners voices could be heard which expressed disillusionment with the structure of the Federation. It gradually came to be recognized that a powerful central organisation could serve the interests of the miners in a better way. There were, however, numerous obstacles to the achievement of this goal. The district officials entertained doubts about their own positions in a centralized regime. A number of district unions, the Durham Miners' Association for example, had vast funds; some had property, and the amalgamation of all unions into one central organisation would have resulted in losses to some of the district unions. A way had to be found whereby the interests of the district unions could be kept intact along with their reorganisation into a central body.

The movement for centralisation began to gather momentum in the early thirties. Looking through the Annual Reports of the M.F.G.B. before it came into its present shape, one finds numerous resolutions and proposals which aimed at some sort of reorganisation of the Union. The district officials were given the assurance that they would not be in a worse position than they were before and the Conference of 1937 found the delegates more realistic in the treatment of the problem of reorganisation. Then followed the Horner-Watson Proposals of 1938. These were not put through because the voting on them by the districts was burdened with many qualifications. The advent of the World War II shifted the attention of the Union leaders from the problem of internal reorganisation to the more immediate task of contributing towards the war effort. But the war also brought about a change by transferring to the national level those problems which were formerly the concern of district unions. By 1943 the Executive of the Union had worked out detailed proposals which provided a compromise between district autonomy and complete unification. The Nottingham Conference in 1944 finally adopted the new rules with some modifications.

The Present Set-up of the N.U.M.

We may now summarize the present structure of the N.U.M. At the top the N.U.M. has close relations with the Trade Union Congress, though the latter does not exercise any formal control over the members of the former. The supreme policy-making body is the National Executive Committee which is elected by the Areas and which exercises a powerful influence on the stand taken by the N.U.M. on specific issues. The President and the Secretary are whole-time officials and the Vice-President is elected biennially by the Conference delegates. Then follow the District or Area Unions. A general Secretary or a President leads the District Union and is generally an individual with a great deal of backing in his own Area. At the bottom are over 800 branches or lodges in which the main officers are: Secretary, Delegate, President, and Treasurer. Generally the lodges are organised on pit basis though sometimes one lodge may cover more than one pit.

Effects of Centralisation

The purpose of tracing briefly the history of the reorganisation movement in the N.U.M. and of indicating its present structure is to show that the tendency towards centralisation has invested increased powers in the hands of the head office in London. The tendency to make agreements on the national level gradually shifted the scene of action from the districts to the centre.

Questions of industrial policy came increasingly into the hands of the central office in London. This also applied to strike action, which could now be officially supported only if a 2/3rd majority of the national vote favoured such a course. It would be difficult to assess the precise amount of change which has taken place in the relative positions of the lodges, the districts and the National Executive Committee. But it seems reasonable to assume that with the shrinkage in the functions of the lodges and the increased strength of the centre, a certain measure of gulf has arisen between the miner in the pit and the National Executive. Occasionally criticisms have been directed at the Executive of losing touch with the miners in the pits[1]. This is one of the reasons why the National Executive, despite its repeated exhortations, sometimes finds it difficult to persuade the strikers to return to work.

The "unofficial" strikes reflect the varying degrees of co-operation which have been reached between the Coal Board and the N.U.M. at different levels. Despite occasional differences, it would be true to say that the extent of cooperation achieved between the Board and the National Executive of the N.U.M. is remarkable. If any forecasts could be made on the basis of past relationships in the industry, it would probably be correct to say that the amount of co-operation and goodwill which now exists at the national level would have been very difficult to achieve under private ownership of the industry. The miners' leaders are conscious of the role which they have played in making nationalisation a reality. When, at the time of nationalisation, consultations took place between the representatives of the miners, the T.U.C. and the Labour Government, the N.U.M. insisted that it must remain a free and independent organisation and not itself take over the administration of the Coal Board

[1] See, for example, the remarks of a delegate from Yorkshire at the Annual Conference of the N.U.M., 1948. He said: "I am a coal-face worker, and I wish to say that some of us coal-face workers think the Executive and our head officials, and most of the Coal Board, have lost touch with the working conditions underground.... Conciliation is all right if you have both got a whip, but if they have taken your whip away from you, while they can still use theirs, then it becomes a travesty".

This was strongly denied by another Yorkshire delegate who said that "it would be totally wrong for this Conference to feel that his contribution to this debate represents the point of view of Yorkshire miners or of the Yorkshire delegation at this Conference". Annual Report, p. 153.

to run the industry. But the N.U.M. also decided that the policy which it would follow would be aimed at making nationalisation a success. Thus, while the Union kept its inherent right to take an independent action in case of sharp differences with the Board, it also recognized its changed functions in a nationalised industry. The N.U.M. leaders, therefore, consider it their responsibility to contribute their utmost in making the industry a success, and, taking an over-all view of their policies, it would be a fair assessment to say that their efforts in this direction have been praiseworthy.

The co-operation which is in evidence at the centre has not so far been achieved at the pits. The numerous small stoppages and restrictions to which we have referred in Chapter III are a clear evidence of this lack of co-operation. The importance of harmonious relations at the pits cannot be over emphasized[1].

We have so far attempted to show that the increased powers of the central organisation of the N.U.M., which reduced the functions of the lodges, have tended to create a distance between the miner and his leaders. The "unofficial" strikes are a manifestation of this trend. Time and again, the rank-and-file of workers have rebelled against the enforcement of agreements which have been arrived at on the national level, thus giving rise to "unofficial" strikes. However, the significance of these strikes should not be over-rated. Most of these are short-lived and are caused by transitory factors which are likely to occur at the present time when the industry is undergoing a great reorganisation. The total loss caused by stoppages and "go-slows" is small, though the output thus lost is vital for the country's export and internal needs.

Another factor which is partly responsible for the numerous "unofficial" strikes, is the delay involved in the settlement of disputes which are submitted to the negotiating machinery.

---

[1] Sir Hubert Houldsworth, Chairman of the N.C.B. while addresssing the N.U.M. Annual Conference, 1953, said: "There is great urgency of endeavour needed to meet the present difficulties. I know that if these difficulties are really understood at the pits, efforts will be made to correct them. It is at the pits that coal is obtained. It is at the pits where there must be understanding. It is at the pits where co-operation is most essential. The joint efficiency committees must help in getting the knowledge of our needs to the pits — it is there where we shall succeed or fail".

The democratic process, which gives ample opportunities to both the parties to present their viewpoints exhaustively before the bodies set up in the industry, necessarily slows down the working of the negotiating machinery. This makes an unfavourable award all the more unacceptable to the workers. While it is proper to remark that the speeding up of the working of the negotiating machinery would be appreciated by the miners and may lessen the number of strikes, it would be very difficult to define the time-limit within which disputes should be settled[1]. Long drawn-out wage bargains tend to exhaust the patience of the miners, who begin to believe that nothing short of the spectacle of a strike would force the attention of their own leaders as well as of the employers on their grievances. However, sometimes "what union members object to is not so much the long months of bargaining as a final failure to achieve the required increase in wages"[2].

National Executive and "Unofficial" Strikes

Generally speaking, the Executive Committee of the N.U.M. is opposed to "unofficial" strikes. The former President of the N.U.M., Sir William Lawther, made it quite clear in some of his Presidential addresses. We quote below two short extracts. Addressing the Annual Conference of the N.U.M., 1948, he said:

> "..... they (unofficial stoppages) are wrong; they are criminal; they cannot be tolerated or excused. Those who indulge in them must, in their less exuberant moments, realise that in an industry where the utmost facilities and opportunities exist for full, frank and free discussion and consultation, their actions benefit nobody, except those, who, if the opportunity presented itself, would drive you back to the depths from which you have risen.

Or again, quoting his own words in the Annual Conference of 1949, he said:

---

[1] *The Economist* wrote: ".... to impose a time limit on the deliberations of wage-fixing bodies, would be an arguable step; clearly it would be undesirable for those claims which involved important points of principle, and had far-reaching repercussions on other section of industry, to be considered, as it were, under duress." July 12, 1947, p. 75.

[2] P.E.P., *British Trade Unionism*, 1949, p. 57.

> On our part we promise you service that is the best any Trade Union can give, but we have also a right to expect that there shall be an end to unofficial strikes. We know the difficulties and sometimes the provocation, but you now have machinery for settling problems as they arise that you never had before: it is a crime against our own people that unofficial strikes should take place, and we advise you in your own interest to watch very carefully those who so readily call on you to strike. They are not your friends; they have other axes to grind than yours. Be on your guard against them.

Not all strikes, however, even though declared to be "unofficial", arouse the Union's antipathy. In many the Union branch officials, and in some, the National Executive, adopt a sympathetic attitude and attempts are made behind closed doors to bring about some sort of *rapprochement*. Sometimes the lack of any clear stand by the Union officials, either for or against the strike, tends to create confusion among the strikers. In such cases, as we shall show in the next chapter[1], the strikers continue to hold out in the hope that sooner or later the strike will be given official recognition. Some of the miners' leaders also feel that, while for the first few years a number of concessions had been yielded to the miners and which have had long overdue, the Board has now gradually been developing a "get-tough" policy which is based on the idea that the miners have had enough and that the time has now come to call a halt to granting any further benefits to the miners.

Suggestions

In the bewildering diversity of the problems which beset the industry and on which differences between the miners and the Board arise, it will be difficult to suggest clearly worked out measures to counter the occurrence of "unofficial" strikes. It must be remembered that, to a certain extent, "unofficial" strikes are inevitable in the present set-up of the Union and in its relations with the Board, which make it difficult for the leaders of the Union to recognise a strike as "official".

It has sometimes been suggested that "unofficial" strikes are a union responsibility, but any such one-sided approach will not provide a solution to the problem. No doubt the Union has to discipline its members a good deal so that the disputes, instead

[1] *vide* The Concessionary Coal Dispute.

of assuming the form of a stoppage, are submitted to the disputes-settlement machinery. A number of such disputes are caused spontaneously and it is doubtful if even the most cleverly designed conciliation machinery would eradicate them. The miners taking part in "unofficial" strikes break their contracts with the Board and also infringe the rules of their own Union. In theory, the Union should penalize the rule-breakers which it can do by withholding from the strikers the benefits to which they are entitled as members of the Union. But apart from not granting strike-pay, the N.U.M. has not tried to penalize the strikers in any other way, though, as already mentioned, the leaders have condemned such strikes. The loss of earnings during the period of the strike is, to a certain extent, made up by the provision of family allowances, national assistance etc.[1] The strikers have been sued for breach of contract, but it is doubtful if the extension of this method would prove effective. The courts may impose fines but their collection, if the number of strikers happens to be large, will present difficulties of a practical nature. It might also create bitterness among the miners towards the Board. A more commendable system is the method of "mitigated penalties" as adopted in Durham. A fine is imposed on the strikers on the understanding that it will be refunded if they do not indulge in irresponsible action for a certain length of time after the strike has ended. The speeding up of the conciliation machinery, so far as it is possible, will also provide an incentive to the miners to submit their disputes to the conciliation machinery rather than take recourse to strike action.

Lastly, it may be emphasized that the "unofficial" strikes, as indeed all strikes, will decrease if the miner in the pit is given a sense of participation both in the running of the colliery and in the affairs of his own union.

Summary

The origin of "unofficial" strikes can be understood against the background of two broad factors, *viz.*, (i) the hostile environment in which the Trade Unions have developed and (ii) the

[1] See *The Times*, July 21, 1954, the article on "Unofficial" Strikes entitled "A Union Responsibility".

increased centralisation in the administration of Trade Unions. In the N.U.M. the scene of power has been gradually shifting from the Districts to the Centre. The workers sometimes indulge in "unofficial" strikes to draw the attention of their leaders to the difficulties which they experience in the pits. But the significance of these numerous, short-lived strikes should not be overemphasized. Avoidance of delay in the settlement of disputes, and giving to the miners a sense of being actively linked-up with the affairs of the Union will reduce strikes.

CHAPTER V

SOME MAJOR DISPUTES

Having analysed the course of conflict in coal-mining in a general way, we now propose to concern ourselves in this chapter with a detailed examination of six important disputes. These disputes have been chosen not only because the resultant loss from them was substantial, but also because their analysis, as we shall try to show, sheds light on some of the important problems in the realm of industrial relations and conflict in the industry. Each dispute is presented in its proper setting, the arguments of the disputants are set out, the course of the conflict is indicated, and, finally, the important issues involved are examined. A wide number of sources have been drawn upon and, wherever possible, evidence is collected from local newspapers to assess the feelings of the strikers during the course of disputes. The chapter ends with a summary giving the main points which emerge from the discussion.

A word may be said about the order in which the disputes are discussed. The first two, *viz.*, the Concessionary Coal (1949) and the Wage (1952) Disputes converge largely on the problem of the wages-structure of the industry; the next two, *viz.*, the Grimethorpe (1947) and Wern Tarw (1951) Disputes bear on the problem of reorganisation of the industry; and, lastly, the Officials' Dispute (1952), which is actually a combined discussion of two disputes concerning the Deputies, brings to light the problem of relationship between the different grades of men employed in the industry. Mention has also been made of a number of side issues without which the picture would have remained incomplete.

The Concessionary Coal Dispute (1949)

Background: The Concessionary Coal Dispute was responsible for the largest amount of coal lost through any single dispute in 1949. The dispute which occurred in the North-Western Division resulted in a loss of about 382,000 tons of coal.

One of the legacies which the Coal Board inherited from the times of the private ownership was the extreme diversity in the wages-structure of the industry. Each district had its own way of paying the wages. The pay-packet of the miner was not restricted merely to the cash he got from the employers; in many cases, it also included various perquisites such as free or concessionary coal, houses at cheap rents, etc. The Board continued to give about 2,000,000 tons of coal every year free to different groups of miners and to supply another 3,000,000 tons a year to other miners at concessionary rates. The granting of these perquisites was governed by agreements with the old employers and the applicability of these agreements was strictly local. When the Board stepped into the shoes of the former owners of the industry, the earlier disparities were allowed to continue. As the *Manchester Guardian* wrote: ". . . . since the old agreements are still faithfully interpreted, ancient generosities and forgotten meanness have been written into nationalisation"[1]. With the exception of the St. Helens area, the Lancashire miners, under the old arrangements, were not drawing any concessionary coal. Even till two years after the advent of nationalisation, this state of affairs was allowed to continue, and the disagreement arose when the Union put forward a demand to rectify this situation. The miners, as a protest against the terms which they deemed to be unjustifiable, placed a ban on overtime working. The strike started when it was alleged that blacklegs were doing the work of the strikers.

The Union's Stand: In the 1947 Conference of the N.U.M., the Executive was asked to seek concessionary coal for all householders who were working in the industry. This was followed by a resolution in 1948 which urged the Executive to press for securing concessionary coal for Lancashire and Cumberland. A

[1] May 6, 1949.

claim was accordingly submitted to the Board asking for coal for the miners in the above-mentioned two areas. This was rejected by the Board. While the question remained unresolved till the end of 1948, a minor agreement was reached at a meeting of the Joint National Negotiating Committee held on August 31, 1948. This agreement concerned the supply of concessionary coal to workers transferred from one colliery to another. It provided that where a man was transferred and, by reason of housing shortage, had to leave his family behind, concessionary coal would be supplied to the family if it were the practice to give concessionary coal at the colliery to which the worker had been transferred. If, however, the custom did not permit the supply of coal at the colliery where the family was left behind, the man would be re-imbursed in cash according to his terms at the new place of work[1]. In July 1948, the Board made a proposal to the Union that an ascertainment should be made of the total amount of free and concessionary coal provided in the whole country, and if the global amount was not sufficient to provide free or concessionary coal to all the householders working in the industry, the Board would be prepared to consider making up the deficiency. The Executive of the Union, while taking note of the Board's proposal, recognised that the question of free or concessionary coal could be considered only as a part of the wages-structure. As Horner put it:

> We were conscious right through the whole business that this would involve us in seeking a revision of district agreements because all allowances, whether they be free coal, concessionary coal, or free houses, have been regarded as part of the wages rates payable within those districts .... Too many considerations have been given in district wage rates based upon the provision of free or concessionary coal to allow us to ignore it. It must become an essential part of the wages structure which in the coming year we shall be compelled to deal with[2].

The Union maintained that since their proposal for the grant of concessionary coal affected more than one District, it became a

---

[1] For the text of the Agreement, see N. C. B., *Memorandum of Agreements etc.*, Part III, 1st January to 31st December, 1948, p. 398.

[2] Quoted from Horner's remarks on Resolution No. 31 on Free & Concessionary Coal, N. U. M. Annual Conference, 1949.

"national" question and should, therefore, be settled through the national conciliation machinery. Accordingly on the 4th March, 1949, the Union submitted to the National Reference Tribunal the issue if the claim made by them in regard to cheap coal for mineworkers could be considered a national question within clause 16 (1) (iii) of the National Conciliation Scheme[1]. The Tribunal ruled that "the question could not intrinsically be considered a national one inasmuch as it deals only with the position in the two districts concerned."[2] It also pointed out that granting concessionary coal to miners in the two districts will be giving them an advantage and will imply discriminatory treatment against the rest. After the rejection of the Union's claim, it became obvious that the District Conciliation Board, tied as it was to the 1944 Agreement which had frozen District rates of pay[3], would turn down the claim. But before the matter could be referred to the District Conciliation Board, the men banned overtime work.

In short, the Union recognised that concessionary coal being a part of the wages will ultimately have to be tackled in terms of the revision of the over-all wages structure. But the difficult nature of the task made an early revision impossible. During the pendency of the finalization of the major wage revision, the Union suggested that the miners in Lancashire and Cumberland should be given free coal.

The Board's Stand: When the first approach was made by the Union to the Board in 1948, the Board was in agreement with the Union to set right the confused state of affairs which existed in regard to concessionary coal. The Board, however, maintained

---

[1] The relevant clause is as under:
"A district question shall be transferred to the National Conciliation Board:
.... (iii) If the National Tribunal upon a reference to it by either side of the Negotiating Committee decides that the question is likely to affect or extend to any one or more other districts or otherwise to assume an importance which will not be confined to the district concerned or seriously to affect the national interest". (N.C.B., *Memorandum of Agreements etc.*, Part II, 1st August, 1946 to 31st December, 1947, p. 149).

[2] Twentieth "Porter" Award, N.C.B., *Memorandum of Agreements etc.*, Part IV, 1st January to 31st December, 1949, p. 436.

[3] See the National Wages Agreement between the Mining Association of Great Britain & the Mineworkers' Federation, given in N.C.B., *Memorandum of Agreements etc.*, Part. I, 20th March, 1940 to 31st July, 1946, para 4, p. 81.

that the question of granting concessionary coal in Lancashire could not be considered in isolation from the problem of concessionary coal over the country as a whole. A scheme which sought to bring uniformity in the coal received by mineworkers would mean lessening the amount of coal that was being given in certain areas. Thus miners in Durham and other Divisions, where the quota of concessionary coal was relatively large, would have to give up a little bit to provide for their less fortunate fellow workers in Lancashire and Cumberland. If the Union insisted in maintaining the district arrangements where they were most favourable, then, pointed out the Board, the Union should also continue with arrangements where they were less favourable. The Board also affirmed that if concessions were to be given in the two districts, the costs of production in those two districts would be substantially raised. In the interests of the consumers and the wider considerations of the industry, the Board was not prepared to take a step which would have raised the costs of production. Commenting on the stand taken by the Board, the *Manchester Guardian* wrote:

> The Board's stand is clearly right, but it is not enough to be right and to remain inactive while sectional selfishness perpetuates an obvious injustice. If the Union cannot agree on fair shares it is the Board's duty as the employers of all the miners in the country to give notice that it intends to remedy matters on its own initiative[1].

It might be worth mentioning here that despite the Tribunal's verdict that the question could not be considered a national one, it speaks of the sagacity of the Board to have agreed to discuss unofficially the question with the representatives of the Union on the national plane, subject to the fact that certain aspects of what obtained in other districts were brought into the final consideration of the matter.

From the above description it is clear that there was no fundamental difference between the approaches of the Union and the Board. Both agreed that the issue of concessionary coal, for a final settlement, will have to be considered in the context of the wages structure of the industry as a whole. The difference

[1] May 6, 1949.

between the Union and the Board was "a difference of timing"[1]. The Union wanted to alleviate the sufferings of the Lancashire and Cumberland miners while the question of revision of the wages-structure was being discussed.

Course of the Dispute: As a protest against the stand taken by the Board, the miners in Lancashire and Cumberland banned overtime work. The ban was placed by a delegate meeting of the Lancashire area of the N.U.M. The strike started when it was alleged that deputies (responsible for safety measures) undertook the work which was normally done by miners during overtime. The feelings amongst the miners had already run high, and the very mention of black-legs, a phenomenon against which the Union had consistently fought throughout its existence, was enough to prompt the workers to go on strike. The Burnley miners claimed that the ban on overtime was broken at Reedley and Clifton pits[2]. About 4,000 miners at 19 pits, near Burnley and at Accrington, struck work, and the number swelled to about 40,000 in a few days. More significant than the number of workers involved was the participation in the strike of the men in the St. Helens area, the only part of the Lancashire coalfield in which concessionary coal was given[3]. This was indicative of the solidarity of the miners. Unfortunately the timing of the strike happened to coincide with the absence of the three leaders of the N.U.M., Lawther, Horner and Bowman, who were away in the United States. This hampered any clear-cut lead from the national leadership of the Union.

Settlement: The final settlement came about in this way. The Board and the Union set up a Joint Committee to work out a scheme "whereby men in other coalfields would accept a reduction in their own entitlement and the Board would bear part of the cost up to about £ 140,000 a year". The majority of men, however, refused to accept any cuts in their quota of concessionary coal and the Board, therefore, decided to spend their share of about £ 140,000 towards providing concessionary coal in the two

[1] Horner's remarks, *op. cit.*
[2] *Daily Dispatch*, May 4, 1949; also *Daily Mirror*, May 4, 1949.
[3] *Manchester Guardian*, May 6, 1949.

coalfields. The amount of coal originally given was 4 tons and 8 cwts. and a rebate of 31s. a ton was allowed on the price of coal supplied. A further revision raised the amount of coal given to 6 tons.

Some Issues Involved: Despite its "unofficial" nature, the strike had great Union sympathy. To substantiate this we quote Horner again. He said:

> Of course we regretted the stoppage which came about, but right from the beginning we have felt that the request of the Lancashire and Cumberland men was justified, having regard to the fact that the Ascertainment system no longer existed and that national minimums had come into being which wiped out the importance which allowances in kind held in previous days[1].

The sympathy of the Union at the national level seemed to have given some wrong impressions to some miners. One miner is reported to have said: "We thought the strike would be official. Now we find it is unofficial, and after drawing thin wage packets this week for last week's work, when the overtime ban was in force, we find that we shall have no strike pay"[2]. In many disputes, though the strike remains unofficial, it carries union sympathy and efforts are made by the Union behind closed doors to reach agreement. It is the obligation "to honour our agreements" which does not permit the Union to support a strike openly.

By bringing into discussion the unequal perquisites which the miners were getting in different areas, the dispute helped to emphasize the need for uniformity in the grant of perquisites. In Durham, some miners were allowed 12 tons of cheap coal per year for each household, or fifteen tons to families with more than four people. If they did not need the entire amount of coal, they could sell it back to the Board at prices which ranged upto 33s. a ton. Similar arrangements for selling back unwanted coal also existed in Northumberland, Yorkshire and the Midlands. The Lancashire and Cumberland miners, in the face of such existing disparities, did what other human beings under the same

[1] *op. cit.*
[2] *Daily Telegraph*, May 7, 1949.

circumstances might have done, though the method of expressing their protest would have been worthy of appreciation if, instead of taking recourse to the weapon of strike, they would have approached the conciliation machinery for settlement.

Connected with the above is another problem. So long as any issue amongst the miners stirs up in them feelings of "we" and "they", the voice of the miners remains one. But when the sectional interests of the miners themselves diverge, the dissension amongst their ranks shows up. It is interesting in this connection to refer to a statement made by the N.U.M. Secretary of the Lancashire Area. He said that even though 100% of the coalfields were sympathetic towards the demand of the Lancashire men, he saw no chances of the strike being declared official. A two-thirds majority needed for the proposal to declare the strike official could not possibly be secured because fourteen-fifteenths of the British coalfields were already getting concessionary coal[1]. Thus, while on the surface the miners' dispute seemed to be with the Coal Board, it actually was with their own fellow-workers in the N.U.M. If the miners in other areas had been prepared to relinquish part of their own quota of coal, the difficulty of the miners in Lancashire and Cumberland could have been solved. One, therefore, fails to appreciate why, when the obstinacy of the more fortunate miners stood in the way of settlement, such a great amount of loss should have been incurred through the strike on this issue. The *Daily Telegraph* commented:

> A strike on such an issue can only be described as frivolous, though it must be recognised that the dispute results from the mishandling by the N.U.M. of the whole question of free coal. If the Union insists on preserving the privileges of the districts which receive too much coal, it cannot expect to claim additional coal for those which receive none or too little[2].

The attainment of uniformity in the grant of perquisites as a part of wages would be an important step towards reducing the possibility of unrest in the industry. This uniformity might be achieved at the expense of a section of the miners and might mean

[1] *Manchester Guardian*, May 9, 1949.
[2] May 7, 1949.

an immediate loss to them, but long-term considerations seem to make this reform an essential one. To conclude this aspect, the sense of social responsibility, which transcends narrow, selfish considerations and which is argued as a great merit of nationalisation, did not make its influence felt in this dispute.

A minor point reflecting on the price policy of the industry was the refusal of the Board to grant concessionary coal in Lancashire and Cumberland on the ground that this would have materially raised the costs of production. As a body which has to balance the interests of the workers in the industry, the consumers of coal and the larger community, the Board has a difficult path to tread. By showing its readiness to settle the dispute but not at increased costs, the Board demonstrated that it was conscious of the great responsibility which devolved on it.

The Wage Dispute (1952)

Background: This dispute refers to a number of stoppages, restrictions and bans on Saturday working, particularly in the Scottish and South Western Divisions, which took place on the rejection by the National Reference Tribunal of a claim submitted by the N.U.M. for a general rise in wages.

On May 15, 1952, the N.U.M. submitted a claim to the National Coal Board for "a substantial increase in wages for all grades covered by the Conciliation machinery — daywagemen and pieceworkers — irrespective of ceilings". This was followed by a subsequent claim in which the Union "desired that an increase of 5s. per shift should be granted to all daywagemen and pieceworkers, irrespective of ceilings, and that the national weekly minima should be increased by 30s. ,making the minimum for adults below ground £ 8 10s. 6d. and that for adult surface workmen £ 7 11s. 6d."[1] In addition to this, there were two supplementary claims put forward by the N.U.M.'s side at the meeting of the National Negotiating Committee. The one consisted of the payment of adult rates to persons above 18 years of age and not 21 years as was the practice. The second concerned the five-day week bonus payment. The practice was that a miner who worked for five shifts in a week was paid for six,

[1] Coalmining Industry Conciliation Scheme, National Reference Tribunal, Claim for Increased Wages, 1952, N.C.B. London, p. 7.

but if he missed one, he lost his pay both for the shift missed and the bonus shift. The Union suggested that a fifth of the bonus shift should be paid for each shift worked.

The whole issue was discussed at the meetings of the Joint National Negotiating Committee held on 26th June and 22nd July, 1952. The parties failed to come to an agreement, and the matter was, therefore, referred to the National Reference Tribunal.

The Union's Stand: The stand taken by the N.U.M. for an increase in wages can be summarized broadly under three heads: first, a rise in wages was necessary to keep the real standard of living of mineworkers from falling; secondly, the mineworkers should rightly participate in the increased productivity which was in evidence in the industry; and, thirdly, an increase in wages would attract an increasing manpower to the industry which would be essential for keeping up the supplies of coal for internal and foreign markets. The Union argued that a more imaginative and broad approach to the whole question of coal had to be adopted. In refusing to grant this increase, the N.U.M. felt that the Board had been adopting policies for wage restraints in a purely mechanical fashion, thereby presenting an approach that was "narrow and sterile" and was oblivious of the wider considerations of Britain's economic recovery in the post-war world. The Union maintained that since November 1947, when the mineworkers had been given their first increase since the Vesting Day, the miners' real standard had registered a decline. This was applicable both to the daywagemen and the pieceworkers. In support, the N.U.M. cited the Interim Index of Retail Prices which had gone up from 101 in October 1947 to 137 in August 1952. The Union admitted the contribution of the Coal Board in raising the productivity through schemes of technical reorganisation, but at the same time stressed that the workers should have a rightful share in this improvement in the shape of higher wages. The output per manshift overall in 1952 had shown an increase of 11% over the figure for 1947. Even though the pieceworkers had been granted increases in wages consequent on the changes in price lists and the flat rate increase granted under the Second Increase in Wages Agreement in 1951, the N.U.M.

maintained that the real standard of living of these workers had gone down, since the increases in wages had not kept pace with the increases in the cost of living. Besides, the pieceworkers had not been allowed to get any extra benefit commensurate with the rise in productivity. The N.U.M. calculated that if the pieceworkers had been allowed a share in the increased productivity and had also been adequately compensated for the rise in the cost of living, their average earnings per shift in May should have been 56s. 5d., and not 50s. 10d., as they then were. The case of the pieceworkers was particularly strong since they were subjected to long periods of absence, caused by high accident rates and industrial diseases. The N.U.M. contended that even though the average earnings of the pieceworkers may have been very much more than other workers, over a period of time the latter were comparatively better-off because of their continuous employment, a feature which was hardly consistent with the dangerous work performed by pieceworkers at the face. The Union strongly deprecated the Board's quotation of earnings which included overtime working, and stressed the fact that their claim was for an increase in the national minima on the basis of the Five-Day week. This, as we shall hope to show later on, was one of the important reasons for discontent amongst the mineworkers, resulting in ban on Saturday working after the National Reference Tribunal had completely rejected the claim of the Union.

Placing the ideal of manpower in the industry at a figure of 750,000 for getting the amount of coal required by the country, the N.U.M. sought to show that unless increases in wages as envisaged in its claim were extended to the mineworkers, the required manpower could not be expected to join the industry. The schemes of technical reorganisation as propounded in the Coal Board's "Plan for Coal" would render impossible any spectacular increases in productivity in the short run, actually a large labour force would be producing only the minimum output. This, the N.U.M. contended, strengthened the case for increased manpower which could only be attracted and, no less important, sustained at a national minimum rate of £ 8 10s. 6d. for underground and £ 7 11s. 6d. for surface workers. If the Board referred to the cost of reforms that had been initiated after the industry had been nationalised, the N.U.M. suggested that such reforms were long overdue and that if they had not been introduced, the industry would have been in a calamitous position. Further, the N.U.M. drew the attention of the tribunal to the hazardous nature of the work, the high rate of accidents despite safety measures and the scourge of pneumoconiosis and suggested that extra care should be taken to take all these factors into consideration before the wage was settled for the mineworkers.

In concluding their case, the N.U.M. stressed the importance of increased production of coal for placing Britain on the road to economic recovery. If Britain could increase the production of coal, it could not only supply abundantly its own industries with power but also increase exports of this important commodity and get in exchange vital imports such as foodstuffs and other raw materials. The increase in production in a short time could be achieved only by getting the additional men required and the pre-requisite of this was the advancement in wages.

The Board's Stand: In rebutting the arguments advanced by the N.U.M., the Board developed its arguments on the following lines.

The Board maintained that the submission by the N.U.M. for an increase in wages was in contravention of clauses 10 and 11 of the Wages Agreement which had been arrived at on 31st December 1951. Clause 10 laid down that for a period of twelve months from the day the agreement was arrived at, the then existing piece rates would continue in operation and no variation should be made or sought to be made in those rates unless the working conditions or methods had undergone a change. The clause also laid down that no variation would be sought in the rates awarded in the then existing operative awards of the district conciliation machinery in the industry or in the district rates. Clause 11 of the same Agreement provided for the appointment of a Joint Committee to consider the existing wage structure of the industry and to suggest methods for working out a more rational structure wherein similar effort could be rewarded by similar returns[1]. The Board, therefore, maintained that the submission of the N.U.M. for a rise in wages was not only an infringement of the Agreement of 1951, but that it would also hamper the task of the Joint Committee which had already started its work in the direction of evolving a more uniform wages-structure. If the claim were granted, the Coal Board suggested, it would result in perpetuating the existing anomalies and thereby complicate further the already difficult task of the Committee.

The Board then considered the wage claim submitted by the N.U.M. in relation to the Interim Index of Retail Prices. It had already agreed to take the cost of living into account while considering wage claims[2]. From 22nd November, 1951, the day

---

[1] The relevant parts of Clauses 10 and 11 of the said Agreement are reproduced below:

"10. *Stabilisation.*

(i) ..... the following clause shall apply and be binding on the Board and the Union: —

(a) "The parties hereto agree that during the currency of this Agreement no variation will be sought in the rates awarded in the existing operative awards of the district conciliation machinery in the coalmining industry or in the district rates.

(b) Further the parties agree that the existing piecework rates shall continue in operation and no variation shall be made or sought to be made in these rates during the currency of this Agreement except in respect of changed methods or conditions of working".

(ii) "Clause 10 (b) above shall operate with effect from the date of this Agreement and for a period of twelve months therefrom or until such time as the Joint Committee referred to in Clause 11 below has agreed revised methods and procedure for the regulation of wages and conditions of pieceworkers whichever period may be lesser.

"11. *Joint Committee.*

The Board and the Union shall appoint a Joint Committee with the following terms of reference: —

"To consider the existing wage structure of the industry with particular reference to pieceworkers and to submit a report to the Joint National Negotiating Committee on the procedure which would be most suitable for the future regulation of the wages and conditions of such workers so as to achieve a more rational wage structure with greater uniformity in wages and emoluments for similar work and effort".

(N.C.B., *Memorandum of Agreements etc.*, Part VI–1st January to 31st December, 1951).

[2] It will be useful, in order to provide the necessary background, to go briefly into history here. The National Reference Tribunal by its 23rd Award had rescinded the War Addition Agreement of 1940. The case leading to the 23rd Award of the Tribunal arose out of a claim submitted by the N.U.M. for varying the formula for determining the addition to wages as laid down in the War Additions to Wages Agreement of March 20, 1940. The important features of the 1940 Agreement we have already mentioned in Chapter III. The union in submitting its claim before the Tribunal suggested that due to

when the wages of the mineworkers were last increased, till May 1952, the Board pointed out, that the Interim Index of Retail Prices had registered an increase of 4.65 per cent. But this rise was also caused by a rise in the price of coal. Since

---

the cessation of the Ministry of Labour Cost of Living Index in 1947 and the issuance of the Index of Retail Prices, the latter should replace the former and any change in the Index of Retail Prices should "have the equivalent effect on wages as each two-point change in the Cost of Living Index would have had in the Agreement unamended". In the case of lower-paid workmen, the Union suggested that the 1940 agreement should be replaced by a negotiated settlement which would provide for consolidation in the wages of all workmen of the existing flat rate payment of 2s. 8d. per shift, increases in the daywage rates, an appropriate increase in the ceilings, which were then 21s. 10d. for surface and 23s. 6d. for underground workers, corresponding to the increase in the daywage rates.

The N.C.B. contended that the War Wage Agreement had become obsolete and should, therefore, be rescinded, that the substitution of the Index of Retail Prices for the Cost of Living Index would be inappropriate, that all the money due to the mineworkers under the War Wage Agreement had been paid, and that if the cost of living had gone up since 1947, the wages and conditions of work also had been considerably improved. Stating that the lower-paid workers were those who were getting only the minimum wage, the Board was ready to increase the minimum wage by 5s. a week so that the minimum for adult surface workers would be £ 5 5s 0d and for underground workers, £ 6 0s 0d. This was inclusive of the skilled shilling, war addition of 2s. 8d., and the nominal value of allowances in kind. The Board also agreed to raise all existing adult daywage rates below 17s. 6d. (surface) and 20s. 0d. (underground) to 17s. 6d. and 20s. 0d. respectively. The Board also offered, subject to certain safeguards, to raise the national minimum wage rates for persons below 21 by 5s. per week instead of the proportionate increases suggested by the Union. The Board calculated that the above-mentioned measures on implementation would cost them a sum of £ 2,250,000 per annum.

The N.U.M. and the N.C.B. were able to find considerable common ground in their discussions in the meetings of the Joint National Negotiating Committee. But there were two points on which no settlement could be arrived at, *viz.*, the definition of "lower-paid workers" and the precise amount of increases in wages that were to be allowed. The matter was, therefore, referred to the Tribunal.

The Tribunal, after carefully considering the whole case, ruled that the War Wage Agreement of 1940 had been rendered obsolete by the cessation of hostilities, ending of District Wage Ascertainments, the termination of the Cost of Living Index and the coming into existence of the Minimum Wage. The Tribunal, therefore, rescinded the War Wage Agreement on the condition that the 2s. 8d. per shift payable thereunder would be consolidated in the current wages. The Tribunal also laid down that all the monies due to the mineworkers under the War Wage Agreement would be deemed to have been paid. It further suggested that while any payment to the lower-paid workers would reduce the differentials, care should be taken to maintain differentials up to a certain extent. It awarded a total sum of approximately £ 3,500,000 to be used for increasing the wages in the industry and left the distribution of the same to the Joint National Negotiating Committee in accordance with the principles which the Tribunal had laid down in its Award (In this connection see the different N.C.B., *Memorandum of Agreements, etc.*, specially Part I, pp. 8–9 and Part V, pp. 596–602).

most of the mineworkers received coal at cheap prices, the rise of 4.65 per cent did not accurately show the extent to which this increase had hit the mineworkers, and for a proper estimate, therefore, adjustments were necessary. Further, the Board pointed out that in granting an advance of 2s. 3d to underground, and 1s. 11d. to surface workers in October 1951, the Board had allowed a rise which was more (by 2.03 per cent in case of underground and 1.85 per cent in case of surface workers) than what was warranted by the rise in the cost of living. Thus part of the rise in the cost of living, which had impelled the Union to submit a claim for wage increase in 1952, had already been covered in the increases granted in 1951. Quoting extensive statistics pertaining to earnings, output per manshift and indices of retail prices, the Board tried to substantiate its contention that the mineworkers had been getting a square deal and that the rise in the cost of living had not outrun the increases in their wages. It produced figures to show that in October 1951 the average weekly earnings in coal-mining were the highest among the heavy industries of the country, and that, with the singular exception of cement, the percentage increase since October 1948 in coal-mining was the highest recorded in any heavy industry.

We have already seen that the N.U.M. had contended that a rise in wages was necessary for improving the manpower situation in the industry. The Board maintained that the figures relating to manpower had shown that the situation was "very satisfactory". Quoting figures for the first 34 weeks of 1950, 1951 and 1952, the Board tried to show that while recruitment had shown a steady increase, wastage had shown a decline. In order to give a comparative picture, the Board also quoted figures of the number of persons employed in some other industries and tried to establish that, in competition with other industries, coal-mining had been able to attract new entrants.

The Board further argued that its financial position did not permit the granting of any increases in wages to the miners. On the strength of figures of the Profit and Loss account for the year 1951 and the first quarter of 1952, the Board estimated that the end of 1952 would reveal a substantial deficit. Despite the existence of a sellers' market, the Board had not been able to balance its accounts; the reserve fund had not been adequate and the wages bill had risen from £ 248.6 millions in 1947 to £ 333.3 millions in 1951. There was thus a significant rise in wage-costs, and the Board pleaded that the granting of the present claim of the Union would have serious consequences on the Board's financial position. It would raise the price of coal by 5s. per ton, thereby hitting a number of other industries which were using coal as an important material in their production processes. The Board referred to the fact that the effect of a rise in wages would have adverse consequences on the economy of the country as a whole. The inflationary forces, in the absence of increased productivity, would be strengthened; Britain would price itself out of foreign markets thereby deteriorating an already unhappy situation of balance of payments; finally, imports of essential raw materials and foodstuffs will have to be cut down, and instead of an improvement in the over-all economic situation of the country, Britain's position would be worsened. As to the difficult and dangerous nature of the work performed by the miners, the Board suggested that this factor had already been taken into account and had been reflected in the differentials which existed in the earnings of the underground and surface workers; it challenged the argument of the Union that the high rate of accidents affected adversely the earnings of the miners, and as a counterblast to the Union's argument that the mineworkers should benefit from the increased productivity in the industry, it mentioned figures to show the extent of mechanisation which had been carried out in the mines at the initiative of the Board and the amount which it had spent, or had proposed to spend, on Capital account for renovating the equipment to ensure increased productivity. While output per manshift in 1951 as compared to 1939 had gone up by 6½ per cent, earnings per shift, over the same period, had increased approximately by 65 per cent.

Finally, on the question of the two supplementary claims lodged by the Union about the revision of the adult age from 21 to 18 years, and the amendment of the Five Day Week Agreement to introduce the payment of bonus of 1/5th on each shift worked, the Board suggested that while the former, if granted, would mean a sharp departure from the existing practice in the industry and disturb the relative earnings of juveniles in coal *vis-a-vis* other industries, the latter proposal would reduce the incentive for regular attendance, thus defeating the fundamental aim which had prompted the drawing up of the Five-Day Week Agreement.

The Award: The Tribunal after considering "the careful and forcible arguments presented" rejected outright the claim of the Union for granting increase in wages to the miners. While admitting that there had been some rise in the cost of living since November 1951 and any possible rise thereafter might go beyond the incomes of those miners who were getting the minimum wage, the Tribunal pointed out that the Cost of Living Index included "weightings" for the cost of fuel and rent. Since most mineworkers received concessionary coal and many had houses on cheap rents, it followed that the rise in the Cost of Living Index did not mean an equivalent rise in the cost of living of the miners.

The Tribunal recognised the increase in output per man shift that had taken place in the industry and, while admitting the role of mechanisation in this direction, gave credit to the miners for the increase in productivity. But, suggested the Tribunal, most of this increase had been achieved before the Agreement of November-December 1951, and, therefore, it was a factor which had already been accounted for in the terms which were arrived at in 1951. On the question of the adequacy of wages, the Tribunal found that with the exception of the surface minimum wage earners, the miners were much better off than their colleagues in other industries[1]. We have mentioned already that the N.U.M. had strongly deprecated the idea of taking into consideration overtime wages in ascertaining the earnings of the miners. The Tribunal, drawing parallels from other industries, pointed out that since overtime wages were included in earnings in other industries, they did not see any reason why there should be a different treatment in the case of coal-mining. The question

---

[1] 24th Porter Award, *op. cit.*, "No other heavy industry showed so great an increase and indeed, whereas coalmining wages in 1938 were well below those of a number of other heavy occupations, by 1947 it had surpassed all its competitors and since then has continued to widen the gap between the earnings of other heavy competitors and its own".

of bonus shift was left by the Tribunal to the parties themselves, and as we shall show later on, the Union brought it up again before the Board. The Tribunal further found that even though some reduction in earnings, caused by accident and illness, must be made in the case of pieceworkers, such loss was not big enough to warrant an enhancement in wages. While agreeing that the consideration of averages might conceal some individual cases of hardship, the Tribunal pointed out that "wages must be based on general and not on individual circumstances".

The Tribunal were not persuaded that the increase in wages could be allowed without a considerable increase in the price of coal. The N.U.M.'s contention, that the export market was prepared to pay 25s. 0d. a ton more than the controlled price in the country, was countered by the Tribunal by pointing out that there was a possibility of reduction in the price of Polish coal or coal supplied from the Ruhr. Any increase in the price of coal exported from the country would, therefore, mean that Britain would lose its markets, thereby giving a rude shock to the country's economy. Further, an increase of 5s. a ton in the price of coal, which would be inevitable if the wage claim were granted, would affect such important industries at home as ship-building, iron and steel, transport and manufacture generally.

But perhaps the most important consideration which weighed with the Tribunal was the fact that any increase in wages at that time would have interfered with the task of the Joint Committee which was trying to work out a more rational wages-structure for the industry as a whole. The Tribunal thought this of supreme importance and hesitated to make a judgment which would have made an already complicated task doubly difficult.

Finally, the Tribunal deprecated the granting of small increases in wages at frequent intervals. The two supplementary claims for the modification of sixth shift bonus and adult age were left to the two parties to decide.

Reception of the Award: The verdict of the Tribunal came as a surprise to the Union. The *Financial Times* wrote: "..... It (the Award) may even have surprised the Board and other employers, who expected an award of 7s. or 8s. in line with other recent concessions to living costs"[1]. The *Sunday Times* hinted at the rather unfamiliar pattern of the award when it said: "The familiar pattern of an exaggerated wage demand, a blank refusal, and a 50–50 compromise fixed by arbitration or conciliation and grudgingly accepted has been broken by the Porter Tribunal's total rejection of the miners' claim for increased wages"[2]. It supported the Award when it said: "To discredit a fore-ordained pattern which stultifies genuine collective bargaining is perhaps no bad thing".[3] The Award was widely discussed in the Press and generally applauded as would be evident from the following quotations.

The Yorkshire Post wrote: "One can sympathise with the miners at the disappointment they are feeling after the rejection of their claim for a substantial increase in pay: at the same time the National Reference Tribunal were right in their decision to refuse an increase".[4] As the *Scotsman* put it:

> Lord Porter, as responsible Trade Unionists as well as employers know, is one of the fairest of our industrial arbiters. It is, of course, true that in their findings the Tribunal pointed out that the miners' minimum compares favourably with that in other heavy industries. But they also declared emphatically that they were in no way bound to conform to the suggestion of wage restraint urged by the Government.[5]

A stronger disapproval of the miners' claim was when the *Wakefield Express* writing under the caption "Time to Cry Halt" said:

> The miners will be "more than disappointed" at the findings of the Porter Tribunal in rejecting their increased pay claim. So says Sir William Lawther, President of the N.U.M. We confess we do not share in that disappointment and we believe this view will be endorsed by the great majority of our readers not engaged in the coal industry — workers in the engineering trades, for example. If Sir William has his ear to the ground he must know that unionists have long since formed the opinion that, in pressing some of their wages claims, the miners were seeking to take unfair advantage of the country's great need for more coal —

[1] November 3, 1952.
[2] November 2, 1952.
[3] *ibid.*
[4] November 3, 1952.
[5] November 11, 1952.

> particularly for export. We give one view expressed to us this week: "The rejection of the claim is thoroughly justified. The miners are the spoilt darlings of industry"[1].

The *Glamorgan County Times* struck a different note when it said:

> .... we feel it is unfair to condemn the men out of hand. Even in our own district there is a tendency among the non-mining section of the community to attribute these developments to "a natural love" of trouble by the miners! We do not seek to condone lightning strikes or any other means of bringing untoward pressure on the general public, but we do feel that the non-mining section of the area should make greater efforts to understand the reactions of the miners — or a certain portion of them — to the tribunal's decision. .... Simplification of the wages structure .... will not satisfy the miners. The Porter Tribunal has admitted that there has been a rise in the cost of living since the miners had their last wage increase and that is a factor that rankles in the minds of the men when they recall that other groups of workers have recorded wage increases whereas they have not[2].

The *Daily Worker* quoted the remarks of Harry Pollitt: "The contemptuous refusal to give the miners a single extra penny 'has implications which will go far beyond the immediate demands of the miners, unless the whole policy of the Tory Government and the National Arbitration Tribunal is immediately challenged."[3]

Though the National Executive of the N.U.M. accepted the award, dissentient voices were heard amongst the miners all over the country. In two Divisions, viz., the Scottish and South-Western, overt action was taken by the miners and stoppages and restrictions of the Saturday working were witnessed. This caused a loss of 61,035 tons in output in the Scottish Division. In the South-Western Division, 34 pits were affected and a loss of 160,269 tons was incurred in production, and in 1953, in the same Division a further loss of 34,090 tons on the same account was recorded. Attendance fell considerably at the week-end shifts in Cambrian Collieries, Clydach Vale (Rhondda)[4]. At the conference at Porthcawl attempts to gain wide support for the

---

[1] November 1, 1952.
[2] November 8, 1952.
[3] November 3, 1952.
[4] *The Glasgow Herald*, November 3, 1952; also *The Daily Worker* of the same date.

unofficial boycott of Saturday work were defeated by an overwhelming majority, but "profound dissatisfaction" was expressed with the Tribunal's award[1]. The conference urged upon the National Executive to press for (a) a fresh claim for an increase in wages; (b) adult rates of wages for youths at 18 years of age; (c) change in the bonus arrangement under the five-day week agreement, and (d) expedition of the settlement of the national wages agreement. It was indicative of the mood of the conference that when the resolution embodying the above clauses was put forward by the Area Executive Council, it was defeated on the ground that it was "too weak". The following rider was, therefore, added and only then the resolution could be carried: "This Conference calls upon the National Executive Committee to conclude these negotiations within a period of one month, and if the results are unsatisfactory a national conference shall be convened, after consultation with the membership, to decide what steps shall be taken to secure our demands"[2]. In Scotland, about 20,000 Fife and Clackmannan miners decided to send some of their representatives to London to urge upon the national authorities of the Union to ban Saturday working unless an immediate concession to their wage claims was made by the Board. Week-end production fell in 12 Fife collieries where workers absented themselves in considerable numbers as a protest against the Tribunal's decision[3]. Other collieries involved in the strike were: Calderhead (Shotts), Cardowan (Stepps), Bardykes (Cambuslang) and Blantyreferme (Blantyre). However, at a conference of the Scottish Area of the N.U.M. held in Edinburgh on November 10, 1952, the lead given by the National Executive was accepted, though it was reported that the discussions were "heated" and "strong resentment" was shown by a section of the members[4]. The strong resentment

[1] *The Daily Telegraph*, November 6, 1952.
[2] *The Western Mail*, November 6, 1952.
[3] *Scotsman*, November 3 and 4, 1952.
An interesting sidelight bearing on the public relations policy of the Scottish Coal Board was the alleged refusal of the Board to give information about the collieries affected and the amount of coal lost through stoppages. See: *The Scotsman*, November 6 and 11, 1952; *Sunday Post*, November 9, 1952; *Glasgow Herald*, November 7, 1952; *Stirling Journal*, November 6, 1952; *Evening Dispatch*, Edinburgh, November 5, 1952; *Evening News*, Glasgow, November 5, 1952.
[4] *Scotsman*, November 11, 1952.

was caused by the fact that the Tribunal had taken into account earnings derived from Saturday working in rejecting the claim of the mineworkers. The miners felt that the working of the Saturday shift was indicative of their patriotic spirit to produce more coal which the country needed and that if this also meant increased income, it was only incidental to their main motive[1]. In some places, even the desirability of continuing to accept compulsory arbitration was questioned. At a meeting held in Neath .... 29 lodges, representing 38,000 miners, unanimously reaffirmed their previous decision to ban coal-filling on Saturdays, and to call upon all the lodges to take whatever possible action to bring about the justifiable wage increase demand, and also to call upon all lodges to send to their executive council a demand to put an end to compulsory arbitration[2].

Settlement: Shortly after the rejection of the claim, the Union submitted a claim for an increase of 15s. a week for daywagemen. The Board, finding that there had been no material change in the circumstances since the Award, rejected the Union's demand, but consented to give an increase of 6s. a week in the underground and surface workers' minima, which would have brought the underground and surface weekly minima to £ 7 6s. 6d. and £ 6 7s. 6d. respectively. The Board, however, made this offer conditional on "standstill" on piece-rates and the continuance of Saturday working. The Union did not accept this offer. Agreement was finally reached and from February 12, 1953, an increase of 1s. a shift for daywagemen, with corresponding increases in weekly minima, which brought the wage for underground workers to £ 7 6s. 6d. and for surface workers to £ 6 7s. 6d., was granted. Specially skilled daywagemen and daywagemen with supervisory responsibilities were granted an increase of 1s. a shift from 30th October 1953. The weekly paid industrial staff also got a weekly rise of 7s. 6d. from the same date.

Some Issues involved: By emphasizing the need for a rational wages-structure in the industry, the Tribunal stressed a fact which

[1] See, for example, a letter to the Editor published in the *Northern Echo*, November 26, 1952.
[2] *The Western Mail*, November 22, 1952.

although it had been appreciated earlier, had not received the attention which it deserved. In view of the importance of this problem it would be worth while quoting the words of the Tribunal. It said:

> The Tribunal have always been conscious of the desirability of a reconstruction of the wage system and in the past have recommended its consideration and conclusion. While that task is being undertaken they are unwilling to interfere with a wage agreement arrived at so recently as that made at the end of last year, and in particular they would hesitate, in the case of an industry which clings so tenaciously to a belief in the necessity of the continuance of the differentials between the remuneration accorded to varied types of work and varying degrees of skill, to make an award which might interfere with those differentials[1].

This is not the place to go into the highly complicated nature of the wages-structure in the industry or to indicate the way in which it has evolved during the course of years[2]. Had the Board not inherited the anomalies from the pre-nationalisation days, it would have faced a much easier task and would have been able to devise a logical system of paying its employees. But the present wages-structure continues to show great disparities from region to region, within the same region and sometimes even at the same seam. *The Economist* wrote: "Wages in coalmining preserve traces of a country's industrial history, much of it unhappy. A given job may be known by scores of different names in different coalfields and collieries; and the wage rates of the men doing it often vary considerably, without much rhyme or reason, even in different pits in the same coalfield"[3]. The problem, we have already seen, is further complicated by various perquisites to which the miners are entitled in different regions and which are not uniform over the country as a whole. In a wage-system

---

[1] *op. cit.*

[2] *vide* Chapter III.

For some difficulties involved in drawing up the new National wages-structure, see:

(i) Arthur Horner's remarks on a National Wages-structure at the Annual Conference of the N.U.M. held at Rothesay, July 7 to 10, 1947.

(ii) *The Sunday Times*, November 23, 1952.

(iii) *The Times*, November, 25 1952.

(iv) *The Economist*, January 10, 1953, "Wages Policy in the Coal", pp. 93–95.

[3] January 10, 1953.

where unreasonable differences exist, the lower paid areas clamour for increases to bring their wages in line with men getting higher sums in other areas. In the mining industry which clings so tenaciously to the sanctity of differentials in wages, the higher paid men may, in their turn, ask for an increase to maintain the relative differences. Thus it may lead to a situation where frequent increases in wages might, in the absence of increased productivity, unleash inflationary forces to the detriment of the country's economy.

The advent of nationalisation bringing with it the unified ownership of the industry prompted both the Board and the N.U.M. to take steps to set right the obvious anomalies. A tendency towards the uniformity of wages was visible even before nationalisation. The Miners' Charter drawn up by the National Executive of the N.U.M. in 1946 had aimed "at the general application of the day-wage system". Standardized wages, it was argued, would create a more contented labour force by ruling out the possibility of unrest which arises from unequal pay for equal amount of work done. They would also simplify wage negotiations, speed up mechanization, and, by introducing a systematic line of promotion from grade to grade, lessen the possibility of conflict[1].

While it is clear that uniformity will infuse some order into the present chaotic wages-structure, we must not forget that standardization has its own defects. The raising of the wages in the lower-paid areas to the levels of the higher paid regions may involve the industry in an expense which may not be justified by the Board's economic position. The levelling out of the differences may also hinder the movement of miners from the uneconomic to the more profitable pits, thus obstructing the Board's efforts to direct labour to the more productive mines. Finally, standardization may take away the incentive from workers who now earn more because they produce more.

Besides the disadvantages of a uniform wage mentioned in the above paragraph, there are numerous difficulties which this measure necessarily involves. While the Union has been intent since nationalisation to infuse greater uniformity, it seems certain

---

[1] *The Times*, November 25, 1952.

that its own members will place a great obstacle to the execution of this reform. The Union will have to make up its mind whether uniformity is to be advocated on an Area, Divisional or National level. The relationship between the wages of the underground and the surface workers will have to be decided upon. The surface workers, who are generally daywagemen, seem to be deeply dissatisfied with the wages of underground workers who have the scope of earning more because they are paid on the piecerate system. But if piecework is to be maintained in the interests of increasing production, — its abolition at present might lead to very serious consequences, — the form in which the payment is to be made will have to be decided upon, i.e., whether payment should be according to the area excavated, tonnage pooling, etc. Further, the payment to faceworkers will have the consequence of applying the same method of payment to the out-bye workers who receive the coal from the coal-cutters. Finally, standardization will also result in increased centralization of negotiations with its possible consequent effect of widening the gulf between the local and the national levels.

From our enumeration of the causes of disputes in Chapter III, we have shown that the wage-issue remains the single most important factor promoting industrial disharmony. While a deeper analysis will no doubt reveal that not all the disputes shown by the Coal Board to have been caused by the wages-factor actually stem from this source, there is reason to believe that a more uniform wages-structure, which seeks to reward equal work with equal pay will, in the long run, lessen industrial conflict and avoid the numerous wranglings which are at present an everyday affair in the industry.

The Tribunal, therefore, by rejecting the claim of the N.U.M. for an increase in wages, which would have made the task of the Joint Committee all the more difficult, forced the industry to focus its attention on a more fundamental problem which lay, and still lies, at the root of industrial disputes in coal mining. The *Financial Times* wrote: "Certain section of the Tribunal's report are interpreted by some of the men as meaning: 'Finish your reconstruction (of the wages-structure) and then see about your wages"[1].

[1] November 3, 1952.

Another aspect which the dispute helped to bring to light was the nature of relationship which existed between the Union and the Coal Board on the one hand, and the Union leadership and its rank and file on the other. After the announcement of the Award, Sir William Lawther, the President of N.U.M., is reported to have said that the miners had drawn "a double blank" by the Tribunal's total rejection of the Union's claim[1]. The miners, according to him, were more than disappointed, they were indignant, at the result[2]. The acceptance of the Award by the Union leaders showed their belief in the settlement of differences through the conciliation machinery existing in the industry. Tribute was paid to the leaders from different sources and credit must be given to them that in the face of some stiff opposition from some of their own comrades, they did not falter. One of the comments was: "Britain's miners have always been in the van of the trade union movement. By accepting the present adverse decision, their leaders have helped to strengthen the principle of arbitration, which is now so well-established and healthy a feature of industrial relations"[3]. The *Manchester Guardian* struck a similar note when it said:

> The good sense which is the real source of trade union strength in this country showed itself to notable advantage yesterday.... Disappointment, particularly over pay, is a potent cause of trouble, and had there been hesitant leadership in either industry there is no doubt that trouble would have occurred. But there has been no hesitancy. Although Lord Porter's Tribunal totally rejected the miners' claim for an extra thirty shillings a week, the miners' leaders have not questioned that the award is binding on them, and they recommended a delegate conference yesterday to accept the rough with the smooth. The delegates responded with a unanimous card vote approving the recommendation[4].

---

[1] *News Chronicle*, November 1, 1952.

[2] *ibid.*

[3] *ibid.*

[4] November 8, 1952. Engineering was the other industry referred to here. The engineers asked for a wage increase to the extent of £ 2 a week, but were offered 7s. 4d. by the employers. Despite considerable opposition which branded the employers' offer as "an insult", the Engineering Unions decided that the offer should be accepted.

This was a contributory factor which inflamed the feelings of the miners. The fact that the workers in the Engineering industry had got an increase at the same time was no comforting thought to the miners. The Railwaymen also got an increase in wages. See, the *Glamorgan County Times*, November 8, 1952.

The *Western Mail* asked the miners to support their leaders and suggested that the main point at issue was the loyalty of the miners to a Tribunal which had been set up by mutual agreement. All those who brought discredit to the Union by breaking their pledges would do immense harm to the industry[1].

One significant fact which emerged out of the course of later negotiations leading up to the final settlement was the change in the bargaining strength as between the Union and the Board. After the complete rejection of the 30s. wage-increase claim, the Union came back with a much lesser claim, but found the opposition of the Board stiffening. As the *Financial Times* put it:

> It cannot have escaped the notice of the miners' leaders that by over-playing their hand in the first place they have sacrificed the advantage they might have got from an earlier agreement, or that by prolonging the negotiations so far they have endangered their own foreign markets. Most of them are old enough to remember the disastrous effects of the loss of overseas markets after the first World War. This experience will surely make the miners more cautious in their demands for the future[2].

Despite these exhortations, widespread stoppages in Scotland and South-Western Divisions showed that a militant section of the miners, whose exact strength it is difficult to assess, continued to defy the national leadership. A certain amount of internal disciplining in the ranks of the Union, therefore, seems to be an important need for keeping peace in the industry.

The Grimethorpe Strike (1947)

Background: The Grimethorpe Dispute in the North-Eastern Division involved the industry in a loss of about 600,000 tons and thus became, till the time of writing, the biggest strike during the period of the public ownership of the industry. The actual stoppage at Grimethorpe started on August 11 and the men finally returned to work on September 15, 1947, thus extending the stoppage to a little more than a month and affecting in all about 63 collieries.

The dispute arose out of the application of the Five-Day Week Agreement to the Grimethorpe Colliery. This Agreement

[1] November 3, 1952.
[2] February 13, 1953.

between the Board and the miners, which had been signed on March 13, 1947, had laid down that the reassessment of the tasks to be performed by a certain number of workers would be taken up over all the pits on a principle of "a fair day's work by the men concerned working throughout the full time below ground, less agreed travelling time and meal times"[1]. The problem of reassessment of tasks was discussed at a meeting between the Divisional Board and the N.U.M. (Yorkshire Area). It was agreed to send a joint letter to every pit in the Division stressing the desirability of reassessment of the tasks in the light of clause 1 of the Schedule to the Agreement which laid down that "the normal working week for underground workers shall be one of five consecutive shifts of 7½ hours plus one winding time". The difficulty arose when this clause was sought to be applied to the Meltonfield seam where it would have resulted in an increased amount of work done by four units of workers. These four units were finishing their work and leaving the pits at times ranging from 5¾ to 6½ hours every day. Having discussed the desirability of reassessment of tasks, the N.U.M. members of the Pit Production Committee decided to place the matter before their Branch meeting. The meeting, however, rejected the idea of accepting an increased amount of work. Thereafter the Disputes Committee considered the matter. The Committee was formed of two Divisional Board's representatives and two representatives of the workers from the neighbouring pits. After holding five meetings and making one trip underground, the Committee unanimously decided that "so long as the faces remained in their present condition, the number of men should be reduced from between two to four at the four faces". This reduction would have increased the stint of each workman by about 2 feet. Care was taken by the Board to direct the Manager

[1] Clause 11 of the Schedule to the Five-Day Week Agreement reads as follows: "The number of men required to perform given work within each shift or the work to be performed by a given number of men as the case may be shall be assessed by agreement between the management and the men concerned or their appropriate representatives as the case may be on the basis of a fair day's work by the men concerned working throughout the full time below ground less agreed travelling and meal times. In case of difference between the men concerned and the management it shall be settled by reference to the pit conciliation machinery. The Union will not countenance any restriction of effort by workmen resulting in failure to perform the work so assessed".

to inform the men about the decision of the Disputes Committee and also to explain to them the method by which it had been arrived at. The Branch Secretary was also asked to explain the position at the Branch meeting.

Course of the Dispute: Despite all these precautions, the workers at the Meltonfield seam refused to agree to this proposal and a strike was staged. Grimethorpe had already experienced a large number of unofficial disputes during the year 1947, but they had not given rise to sympathetic strikes in the neighbouring collieries. On August 26, however, it was announced by the Regional Coal Controller that all the strikers were considered to have terminated their contracts and if they wanted to come back, they would be required to sign up new contracts. This resulted in a number of sympathetic strikes in the two neighbouring pits[1]. Gradually the strike spread to many more collieries and it was estimated that by August 29, there were 30,000 men at 16 pits involved. On August 30, the General Secretary of the N.U.M., Arthur Horner, addressed meetings of the workers in the area and tried to induce them to go back and try the new stint for a few days. This was on condition that the Board waived the signing of new contracts. The Board agreed to this proposal and intimated that the workers who came back by a certain date would not be called upon to sign new contracts. The date was extended by a fortnight. But the strikers were adamant and refused to come back. A number of mass meetings were organised by the Yorkshire Area of N.U.M., and at one of these the Minister of Fuel and Power addressed the workers. These meetings had no effect on the strikers. Ultimately it was agreed that the men should return to work and a Fact-Finding Committee be appointed to go fully into the matter. Since the condition of the faces had deteriorated during the cessation of work, the Divisional Board, on the suggestion of the N.U.M. (Yorkshire Area), agreed that as many men as were needed should be employed at the faces. The men returned to work, but when the faces had returned to normal conditions, the men again refused to work the extra stint. Fearing that insistence on an increased stint might lead

[1] *Labour Research*, October 1947, Vol. XXXVI, No. 10.

to the repetition of the strike, the Board did not force the issue. It decided to rely on negotiations with the N.U.M. to settle the matter amicably. At a joint meeting of the Board and the N.U.M. (Yorkshire Area), the miners' representatives suggested that due to the unduly long time taken in haulage arrangements, the workers were not prepared to work the extra stint. After enquiries it was found that "the excessive amounts paid as waiting time were not due to faults in the haulage system but to the fact that at this colliery, from 1942 onwards, there had been a practice for overtime to be paid for all stands, no matter how short the period of such stand"[1]. The settlement of the dispute was postponed to the next year when the N.U.M.'s representatives hoped that they would be able to persuade the workers at Grimethorpe to work according to the report of the Disputes Committee. The Board agreed to this[2]. After this, it appears that no further developments took place and the issue was left where it remained at the close of 1947.

Some issues involved: This dispute brought out three important issues. First, it illustrated the delicate balance which has to be maintained between schemes of reorganisation and the men who have to execute them. All efforts were made by the Board and the Union officials to end the dispute amicably, care was taken both by the Manager and the Branch Secretary of N.U.M. to explain to the workers affected the reasons why and how it had been decided to increase the stint. The miners' leaders, even the Minister of Fuel and Power, addressed the meetings of the workers. But all these efforts bore no fruit and the strikers stayed away from work. The reason perhaps lay in the explanation given by *The Economist.* While applauding the vigour with which the North-Eastern Divisional Board had been trying to execute its schemes in the technical field, *The Economist* wrote: "It is possible that the Board have been going too fast for the men, and that management has been treating the miners too much as digits set to work exciting new cutters and conveyors, and has been attempting too little to carry them along as human beings"[3].

[1] N.C.B., *Annual Report and Accounts for 1947*, p. 20.
[2] This description is based largely on the details given in the N.C.B., *ibid.*, pp. 18–20.
[3] September 13, 1947.

Closely allied to the point made out in the above paragraph is a second one. Howsoever elaborate the conciliation machinery may be, its success, especially in the case of miners, will depend upon the intelligent flexibility with which it is applied to particular cases. The atmosphere of the mines is considerably different from that of factories. While in the latter, the uniformity of working conditions generally permits the application of set rules, in the cases of mines, where local conditions vary widely, any rigid scheme might arouse resistance and lead to strikes. Though the Board was technically right in its stand and could have held out, it would only have worsened the situation. "It is doubtful", wrote *The Economist* "if the fluid atmosphere of human relationships can be settled by the rigid application of machinery and principle"[1].

This brings us to our third point. The dispute was the first major outburst of the workers against the schemes drawn up as a result of negotiations carried on on a national level. There is no denying the fact that infusion of uniformity in wages, working conditions, hours of work, etc., will necessitate the discussion of these topics at the national plane, but it seems equally certain that, unless very carefully designed steps are taken, there might arise a great danger of centralisation which may create a gulf between the miner in the pit and his own representatives and the Coal Board in London. This partly explains the scant respect which the miners showed in this dispute towards the national agreement. Since, however, national agreements appear to be the only course to rid the industry of its heterogeneity, the crux of the problem lies in imparting an elasticity to national agreements in order to adjust to special local conditions. This will mean granting a greater autonomy to the officials at the Area and Pit levels. This will also mean granting an increased participation to the workers in the industry. *The Economist* condensed the problem when it wrote: "The real issue which is being fought out at Grimethorpe.... can be summed up as a struggle between rationalisation and syndicalism"[2]. Many miners seemed to have been under the impression that the advent of nationalisation will lead to workers' control.

[1] *ibid.*
[2] September 6, 1947.

But when this did not come about and when, what is more, they found themselves facing the same managers with whom they had fought during pre-nationalisation days, they were disappointed. In executing schemes of reorganisation it should be essential to take the workers in confidence not only at the Divisional, but also at the Area and Pit levels. It is quite likely that had due flexibility been given to the application of the National Agreement and greater freedom accorded to the Area and Colliery Managers to make decision, the trouble at Grimethorpe might have been avoided.

The Wern Tarw Dispute (1951)

The largest amount of loss during the year 1951 was caused by the strikes which were staged as a protest against the proposed closure of the Wern Tarw Colliery in the South-Western Division and which affected 29 collieries. About 115,177 tons of coal were lost on account of this strike.

Background: The trouble arose after the Board decided "because of approaching exhaustion and increasing difficulty of working due to geological conditions" to close Rhondda No. 3 seam at Wern Tarw[1]. This decision was arrived at after discussions had had taken place between the Board and the N.U.M. at Pit, Area and Divisional levels. The closure threatened to render redundant 87 men, 77 underground and 10 surface workers, and alternative employment was provided to them at Llanharan colliery. After the list of the men who were to be transferred had been agreed upon on the pit level, it was found that 10 men had already left the colliery. The Board, however, thought it necessary to adhere strictly to the original number of 87[2]. It was this later step which brought the matter to a head and resulted in strike. The miners maintained that while they had reluctantly agreed to the transfer of 87 men to another colliery, the increase of 10 more people amounted to a breach of agreement[3].

The Strikers' Stand: Though the immediate factor, according to

---

[1] *Western Mail*, June 15, 1951.
[2] *ibid.*
[3] *South Wales Echo & Evening Express*, June 12, 1951.

the spokesman of the Wern Tarw Lodge, was the increase in the number of men transferred from 87 to 97, the strikers also challenged the contention of the Board that the Wern Tarw colliery was nearing exhaustion and that it was threatening to become unremunerative. The strikers' mood on this point was amply represented by a statement which was circulated by the Wern Tarw Lodge Committee among miners at other pits. It said:

> Rather than provide pay and conditions to attract enough Welsh lads the Board is trying to solve its manpower problem by closing collieries, transferring miners, and introducing Italian labour. Districts in our colliery have been systematically "murdered" to establish a case for the Board. This is a threat to the whole of South Wales. Who is to be next on the list? It may be you. It is time to put a stop to this practice. Only a stand can halt the Coal Board[1].

The case of a few more collieries was cited by the Lodge officials to demonstrate that the "policy of the N.C.B. is deliberately to close collieries where there are reasonable conditions prevailing to transfer men to collieries where they are going to worsen conditions"[2]. The Lodge officials, in support of their contention, further pointed out that there were seven new seams of coal at the colliery which were untouched, and which, if worked, could provide employment to those who had been rendered redundant and give to the colliery a bright future. Besides, alleged the Lodge officials, a by-product plant which had cost £ 500,000 to erect and which had not been extensively used was being dismantled[3]. The Lodge officials protested in Cardiff against the proposed closure of the colliery, but the executive council of the South Wales area of the N.U.M. decided that they could not interfere in the matter[4].

Besides the above, the Lodge at Wern Tarw thought that an important matter of principle was involved in the dispute. They alleged that by transferring workers from one colliery to another, the Board was trying to solve its manpower problem. They

---

[1] *Manchester Guardian*, June 22, 1951.
[2] *South Wales Echo and Evening Express*, June 5, 1951.
[3] *ibid.*
[4] *ibid.*

believed that that was not the correct way of solving the problem of manpower shortage which called for more fundamental remedies. Higher wages, better working conditions and general conditions should be made attractive enough to invite more workers to the industry. A further objection arose from the impending fear of a reduction in the earnings of men who were transferred, partly because unfamiliar working conditions could have meant lesser production and, therefore, lesser earnings for them, and partly because it was alleged that the wage rates were lower at the Llanharan Colliery as compared to Wern Tarw. This latter allegation was challenged by the secretary of the Llanharan lodge[1]. The workers transferred also feared that they would be called upon to accept lower grades and in case of retrenchment would be the first to be discharged from their new place of work.

The Board's Stand: The Divisional Board, on the other hand, maintained that the closure of the colliery had become inevitable due to exhaustion and the increasingly difficult conditions of working. They further argued that the decision to take the step had been arrived at after full consultations not only on the Divisional level, at which Wern Tarw Lodge was represented, but also at the pit level. They, therefore, failed to see why a step which had been mutually agreed upon by both the parties should be so stubbornly resisted by the workers and the Lodge officials. Last but not the least, the Board showed its determination to keep up its right of reorganizing the industry on more efficient lines. Reorganisation of the industry was absolutely essential and this was bound to involve the overriding of local by national interests. Even when the workers were rendered redundant, they were provided alternative employment and, the Board pointed out, it was better than having no employment at all.

Course of the Dispute: Widespread strikes were witnessed in the South-Wales coalfield and by the time final settlement was reached, 29 collieries and 2 Central Washeries had been rendered idle in sympathy. It was decided at pithead meetings at Wern

[1] *Western Mail,* June 25, 1951.

Tarw colliery to stage a strike from the 6th of June 1951. At a special meeting held at the Lodge, invitations were issued to adjacent lodges to lend support to the strikers. The Lodge secretary affirmed that co-operation in the effort to put an end to the Board's action would be sought from sister lodges and an attempt would also be made to force the executive council to recognize the strike as "official"[1]. Very soon the strike spread to adjacent areas and in addition to the 700 miners who had stopped work at the Wern Tarw colliery, various pits in mid-Glamorgan area also joined in the strike. This development followed a meeting at Bridgened of the Llantrisant and District Joint Lodges of the N.U.M. Following a pithead meeting at another colliery — Coedely, Tonyrefail — several hundred workmen returned home. The production of the South-Wales coalfields during the first week of strike recorded a drop of about 46,000 tons[2]. The case of the Wern Tarw strikers was explained to the workers at nearby collieries through leaflets and speakers. Workers at Newlands, Aberbaiden and Pentre also struck work in sympathy[3]. By June 23, the *Western Mail* reported, 23 pits in the Division were out, involving more than 9,000 miners, and had caused a loss of about 60,000 tons of coal[4]. This loss had gone up further by the time the workers' delegate conference held in Cardiff on the 29th June had voted by a decisive majority to support their executive council's recommendation to accept the Board's decision to bring an end to the dispute[5].

Settlement: While these stoppages had been witnessed at a number of pits and substantial amount of coal was being lost, the South Wales Area President of the N.U.M. said in unequivocal terms that the stoppages were "unofficial and totally unwarranted"[6]. Declaring that the Coal Board had decided upon the closure in accordance with the joint decision of the representatives of the Board and the miners, the President of the South Wales Area of N.U.M. said: "We, therefore, call upon

---

[1] *South Wales Echo & Evening Express*, June 5, 1951.
[2] *South Wales Echo & Evening Express*, June 12, 1951.
[3] *Daily Worker*, June 13, 1951.
[4] June 23 and 25, 1951.
[5] *South Wales Echo & Evening Express*, June 29, 1951.
[6] *Western Mail*, June 16, 1951.

the workmen who are now on strike to return to work immediately as the policy being pursued by them is contrary to that laid down by the union after lengthy consultation with its members on the question of reorganisation of this industry"[1]. Apparently starting from a rather trivial cause, the dispute at one time threatened to split the Union in South Wales into two camps. This cleavage was visible at the very start of the conference which had been called at Cardiff to discuss the unofficial strike. The viewpoint of the executive council was that the dispute should be discussed as a part of the over-all problem of reorganisation of the industry in the South-Western Division, but the supporters of the strike wanted that the entire discussion should be devoted to the Wern Tarw colliery. The two hundred delegates went back from Cardiff to their respective lodges "to find out whether their members would support the miners' leaders or the unofficial strikers over the Wern Tarw issue"[2]. A further conference was to be called and, pending decision, all miners on strike were asked to go back to work. The strikers' leaders at Wern Tarw expressed their resolution to abide by the decision of the recall conference. Later at the recall conference, the majority voted in favour of the support of their executive council's recommendation to accept the Board's decision to transfer men from Wern Tarw to Llanharan colliery. The result of voting was: 56,100 in favour of the acceptance of the Board's decision, and 39,600 against the acceptance[3]. This put an end to the strike. Despite the Area President's statement that the vote was a decisive one and that it amounted "to a vote of confidence in the men's elected leaders"[4], the minority votes were substantial. This was a clear evidence of the fact that opinion on the issue was sharply divided and that the Executive had no easy task in carrying with itself the rank and file of the members.

Some issues involved: The dispute brought out three important issues which we shall presently discuss. First of all, by resisting the transfer of the miners from a colliery which, according to the

---

[1] *ibid.*
[2] *Western Mail,* June 25, 1951.
[3] *South Wales Echo & Evening Express,* June 29, 1951.
[4] *ibid.*

Board, was nearing exhaustion, the strikers brought into sharp prominence the difficulties which are inherent in any scheme of reorganisation, a point to which we have already drawn attention while discussing the Grimethorpe dispute. It is beyond our scope to comment on the technical aspect which gave rise to disagreement — whether the colliery was nearing exhaustion or not. Whatever be the case, the fact remains that whenever transfer of workers is necessitated by a scheme of reorganisation, difficulties are likely to arise. These difficulties can be largely overcome by giving a complete explanation of the schemes in hand to the workers at all levels. This appears to us to be of very great importance since, in our opinion, disputes arising from changes caused by reorganisation schemes might become increasingly frequent. Technically the industry is still in an unsatisfactory state. Many pits which have seen their best days are still working and the Board is incurring losses on them. The Union has several times pledged itself to support the closure of such pits, to replace them by modern ones and to help to concentrate miners in the best possible pits. But concentration raises serious problems. Tension may arise between local and transferred workers. When a pit is closed it is estimated that about 10% of the labour force cannot find work at the new pit; either because of age or partial disablement, some workers are fit only for tackling lighter jobs. In a sense, therefore, the resistance to closing is partly "the healthy instinct of the strong to defend the weak — the non-transferable — and will only be overcome if proper provision is made for them". In order to solve this problem, the Union had made approaches on three lines: (i) Compensation for a year for men who have been rendered idle due to closure; (ii) Introduction of pensions at 55 to help with the problem of the older men; and (iii) Training for alternative work to be provided for the disabled. The Board and the N.U.M. were finally able to draw up an Agreement providing a scheme whereby "compensation ..... shall be payable to persons rendered redundant as a consequence of the implementation of reorganisation and reconstruction projects"[1].

[1] For full details, see the Agreement given in N.C.B., *Memorandum of Agreements etc.*, Part III, 1st January to 31st December, 1948, pp. 400–403. Also: N.C.B., *Report and Accounts for 1948*, pp. 43–44.

As expounded in the "Plan for Coal", the Board has in hand a scheme for the reorganisation of the industry, and as the programme proceeds, increasing resistance from the workers may be expected. Technical reorganisation involving change in work-patterns is likely to be resisted anywhere, but the sociological structure of the mining societies is likely to make this resistance still more serious in the coal industry. The fact that the workers have been, by the force of their leaders, talked into accepting a certain proposal, makes them at best unwilling partners in a new venture. The Wern Tarw dispute showed this point beyond doubt. The N.U.M. had pledged itself to the policy of reorganisation, actually the Union was reported to have called for an even greater expenditure on the reorganisation of the coalfield than the £ 97 million earmarked for the South-Wales coalfields in the Board's "Plan for Coal"[1]. But when the impact of the reorganisation scheme made itself felt in the shape of the transfer of miners, acute resistance from the lodges was witneessd. The logical conclusion which can be drawn from this is that the workers at the pit concerned gave their consent unwillingly and were somehow not convinced of the desirability of the measure. When the slightest pretext in the shape of the disputed number of 87 presented itself, they struck work. It is, of course, not possible to lay down any degree of willing acceptance which should be attained and without which the scheme of reorganisation should not be put into operation. Much will depend upon the local leadership of the union and upon the tact and care which officials of the Board and the Union bring to bear upon the issue.

Closely allied to the first is another problem, the problem of human considerations in schemes of reorganisation. It is one of the distinct advantages of nationalisation that rigorous economic logic can, up to a certain extent, be tempered by human considerations. While the latter are of importance and should, therefore, be given proper weight, they may not always be compatible with considerations of economy and efficiency[2]. Here again, if economic considerations are to predominate — which

[1] *South Wales Echo & Evening Express*, June 22, 1951.

[2] Such a situation arose in February 1954 at the Northfield Colliery, Shots, in Scotland, where the closing down of a declining coalfield would have resulted in ruining a thriving community life. See *Manchester Guardian*, February 20, 1954.

should not necessarily mean that human factors should be completely ignored — the workers have to be taken into the fullest confidence. To quote from the *South Yorkshire Times:*

> The State is not a sentimental employer..... It is clear that the future history of mining as of any other nationalised industry, is bound to contain some chapters of stern realism. When these come along the men engaged in the industry will be expected to make their contribution towards the efficacy of changes and reforms. There are signs that this lesson is being gradually learned, but the intransigence in South Wales reveals that there are some backward pupils"[1].

The point contested by the strikers, when placed beside the issues for which the workers had fought before the coming of nationalisation, showed the increased strength and prestige of the miners. Before nationalisation an important item in the policy of the Miners' Federation was the insistence on the "right to work". But the Wern Tarw dispute showed that the "right to work" having been achieved, the strikers went a step further and demanded "the right to work where we like"[2]. Set against the background of the pre-nationalisation days when redundancy meant the workers going on the dole, the position now shows considerable change to the advantage of the miners.

Lastly, the dispute showed clearly that a substantial minority still looks to the weapon of strike as an effective means of settling its differences with the Board[3]. Despite the repeated exhortations of the Area Executive of N.U.M. to the strikers to return to work, the workers did not respond. The voting at the recall conference showed that old habits die hard. The change-over from a position where industrial relations were governed by feelings of class war to a situation where the union is called upon to play a more conciliatory role, is not easy. In this connection it might be interesting to quote the statement which was attributed to the Lodge Secretary of the Wern Tarw colliery when the dispute had commenced. He was reported to have said that "the traditional fighting spirit" of the South Wales miner had now been aroused, and would ever present a

[1] June 30, 1951.
[2] *South Wales Echo & Evening Express*, June 28, 1951.
[3] See also Chapter VI.

challenge to the Board both on questions of closure and on other issues[1]. This presumably summed up the stand taken by the minority who voted for the continuance of the strike. The *Western Mail* commented: "If this is, indeed, the spirit in which the Coal Board work is to be regarded then the miners may as well scrap nationalisation"[2].

The Officials' Disputes (1952)

Under this heading we propose to discuss briefly two strikes staged by the Deputies. The first was a strike in the North-Eastern Division. It was caused by dissatisfaction with progress of negotiations for a wage increase, hit 18 collieries and resulted in a loss of about 73,000 tons of coal. The second occurred in the South-Western Division as a protest against the Divisional Board's offer under the New National Agreement for officials, affected 51 pits and caused a loss of more than 60, 000 tons.

Background: Before discussing the disputes, it is necessary to show the position of the National Association of Colliery, Overmen, Deputies and Shotfirers, in relation to the Coal Board and the N.U.M. In 1947, when negotiations were being carried on by the Board for recognizing the organisations representing the various grades of workers and officials, the N.A.C.O.D.S. claimed that it should be recognized as a representative body of Overmen, Deputies and Shotfirers. The Board found that the N.A.C.O.D.S. could speak for most of the Deputies and it was, therefore, decided that this organisation should be recognized as representing the Deputies and conciliation machinery should be provided accordingly. The case of Overmen and Shotfirers was, however, different. Both the N.U.M. (and its newly-affiliated body called the National Federation of Colliery Officials and Staff) and the N.A.C.O.D.S. had a number of Shotfirers and Overmen as their members, and the Board, therefore, recognised both the organisations, the N.U.M. and the N.A.C.O.D.S., as the negotiating bodies for these two grades. During 1948, negotiations continued between the Coal Board and the N.A.C.O.D.S., as the latter

[1] *Western Mail,* June 30, 1951.
[2] *ibid.*

continued to claim that it alone was competent to speak on behalf of Overmen and Shotfirers. The Board did not agree to this and the question remained unsolved. In the meantime, unsettled questions continued to be discussed without any settled procedure. It was because of the absence of any definite procedure that the joint submission in December 1947 by the N.U.M. and the N.A.C.O.D.S. for an increase in the wages of Shotfirers was, with the consent of the Board, decided to be referred to the National Reference Tribunal[1]. In Scotland, however, the Divisional Board was able to make conciliation agreements covering Overmen and Shotfirers with N.A.C.O.D.S. and N.U.M. jointly, and for Deputies, with N.A.C.O.D.S. alone[2]. Though for all practical purposes the N.U.M. and the N.A.C.O.D.S. continued to represent jointly certain grades, there was no doubt that tension existed between the two organisations.

Strike in the North-Eastern Division: The trouble arose when during the course of negotiations between the Board and the N.A.C.O.D.S. about the terms and conditions of employment of the Deputies, the Deputies refused the Board's offer of a weekly wage of between £ 14 and £ 16 10s. The actual rates were to be settled by the Divisions according to local circumstances. The rank and file of the miners thought that this offer was reasonable and should have been accepted by the Deputies[3]. The Deputies had a number of other subsidiary grievances. They wanted that they should be regarded by the Board as being employed "on the same stipulated shift basis as the miners and not to be on call"[4]. They also claimed earnings at least equal to the average earnings of Yorkshire underground workers. According to the figures quoted in the *Yorkshire Post*, in the first quarter of 1952 the average earnings of the underground workers in Yorkshire had risen from 45s. 3d. to 46s. 11d. a day, which was 10s. above the Deputies' and 16s. 7d. above the Shotfirers' rates[5].

[1] See the Memorandum of Agreement made on 3rd March 1948 between the N.C.B. on the one part and N.U.M. & N.A.C.O.D.S. on the other. See also: The Sixteenth Porter Award (N.C.B., *Memorandum of Agreements etc.*, Part III, 1st Januany to 31st December, 1948, pp. 328–336).

[2] N.C.B. *Annual Reports* for the years 1947, 48, 49, 50, 51 and 52.

[3] *Yorkshire Post*, June 19, 1952.

[4] *ibid.*

[5] *ibid.*

While there was dissatisfaction amongst the Deputies over the wage rate claimed, the immediate factor which caused the strike was the delay in negotiations. The Deputies pointed out that negotiations had been going on since their Association made a claim on their behalf for a 10s. a day increase in October 1951. Thus about 34 weeks had elapsed and still there was no guarantee forthcoming from the Board. Commenting on these protracted negotiations, the *Sheffield Telegraph* wrote: "Among the general public there is an uneasy feeling that the claims of Colliery Deputies do not receive the swift attention accorded to the claims of other mineworkers. It is the fate of the Deputies, it seems, always to be at the end of the queue. Their impatience can, therefore, be understood, but the action of the Yorkshire Deputies can only be condemned"[1].

Strike in the South-Western Division: The other dispute occurred in the South-Western Division after an agreement had been arrived at between the Board and the N.A.C.O.D.S. concerning the terms and conditions of employment of Deputies[2]. We have seen above that while the range of payment to Deputies Grade I was agreed upon as between £ 14 to £ 16 10s. a week, the actual amount to be paid was left to be settled by the Divisions. In the South-Western Division, the Board offered to the Deputies a wage of £ 14 a week, the minimum amount which could be paid under the new Agreement. The Deputies in the Division resented this and pointed out that they would be getting less than they were drawing before the new Agreement came into operation. Under the new Agreement the Deputies were to be paid an upstanding wage for each week worked and this precluded the possibility of any additional payment for week-end or overtime work[3]. The Deputies found the withdrawal of all previous allow-

---

[1] June 19, 1952.

[2] For a full text of the Agreement, see N.C.B., *Memorandum of Agreements etc.*, Part VII, 1st January to 31st December, 1952, pp. 384–411.

[3] The relevant clause on wages and its agreed interpretative note in the Agreement read as follows:

"Part B-Wages.

Clause 5.

"5. Deputies Grade I and II shall be paid an upstanding weekly wage for each week worked without any additional payments in respect of overtime or week-end work. (See overleaf).

ances a bitter pill to swallow. Besides, in the South-Western Division due to geological conditions, there was the water hazard to contend with for which the Deputies were paid an extra allowance. In short, the Deputies in this Division found that the new minimum offer, which became the maximum and which did not permit the payment of any allowances, would have meant, on the whole, a lesser wage than what they were already getting. They contended that local circumstances had not been carefully considered in the discussions at Cardiff[1]. There was also the grievance, though not expressly mentioned, that while Deputies in the South-Western Division had been offered the minimum, those working in English coalfields would be getting nearer the maximum figure.

The Divisional Coal Board, on the other hand, maintained that the average of the Deputies' wage for the South Wales coalfield, including overtime, only amounted to £ 11 15s. 9d. a week and that its offer of £ 14 was, therefore, reasonable. To the objection that Deputies in the English coalfields would get more, the South-Western Coal Board might have retorted that "the English coalfields are much more profitable than the South-Wales area and that it could not reasonably be expected to offer more until its finances justified a bigger salary"[2].

In this case also, a contributory factor was the delay in the negotiations before the drawing up of any final agreement. After about 9 months of bargaining it was "little wonder that... the officials were exasperated and in a mood to indulge in strike"[3]

Some issues involved: A special problem involved in these two strikes arose out of the key positions which the Deputies hold in the industry. A cessation of work by these officials naturally renders idle a large number of miners who, in the absence of persons doing

Note:
"(i) The Agreement provides that henceforth Deputies Grade I and II shall be paid an upstanding weekly wage without any additional payments in respect of overtime or week-end work. The weekly wage is an all inclusive one and no payments of any description whether in the form of allowances (other than coal and houses where applicable), bonuses, gifts, or otherwise are to be made in addition to the weekly wage".

[1] For an expression of the Deputies' viewpoint, see: *Colliers' Mail,* September 10, 1952.

[2] *Glamorgan County Times,* August 30, 1952.

[3] *ibid.*

the safety work, cannot continue with their normal duties. Thus a strike by the Deputies which does not carry the sympathies of the miners, inevitably antagonizes the latter and is bound to create tension amongst them. During the strike in the North-Eastern Division this tension assumed serious dimensions. While the Deputies were on strike, the Yorkshire Area Council of the N.U.M. placed before the Coal Board a plan to break any such future strikes. About 800 underground officials had rendered idle about 22,000 miners, a situation which the miners could not tolerate. The N.U.M., therefore, suggested that miners holding Deputies' certificates should take the place of those on strike. The plan also suggested that many more men should be trained for this purpose so that in case of such strikes occurring again adequate reserves could be made available. The N.A.C.O.D.S. did not take kindly to this strike-breaking device by the N.U.M. As an example of the friction between the two organisations, we shall quote two statements. The Yorkshire General Secretary of the N.A.C.O.D.S. said: "Any scheme to break strikes by our members put forward by the N.U.M. will contravene the Coal Mines Act". On the other hand, the Vice-President of the N.U.M. said: "We cannot tolerate any longer a position in which a handful of officials have tens of thousands of miners at their mercy. Disputes involving the Deputies have involved our members in losses of wages, bonuses and the guaranteed wage on a number of occasions"[1]. The inconsistency in the N.U.M.'s stand can immediately be visualized if we recall the course of the Concessionary Coal Dispute, when workers belonging to the N.U.M. staged a strike on the ground that their work was being done by the Deputies.

By showing the cleavage which existed between the two workers' organisations, the disputes demonstrated the rather important fact that the problem of industrial conflict in the coal industry is not merely a problem of the Coal Board *vis-a-vis* the N.U.M. There are occasions when the relations between the organisations of different grades of workers can have important repercussions on the state of industrial peace in the industry.

Allied to the problem of relations between the unions of the

---

[1] Both statements were quoted in *Daily Telegraph*, June 23, 1952.

various grades of workers is the relative neglect of the other organisations as compared to the N.U.M. True, the N.U.M. is the most massive and representative organisation of the workers in the industry, but as was clearly revealed by the strikes discussed above, discontent amongst the other organisations can involve the industry in substantial losses. As the *Daily Telegraph* wrote: " ..... the members of a small and far from popular body may be treated with salutary firmness, but not the members of the great Union whose goodwill the Coal Board must retain ..... It is painfully obvious that in the mining industry the big Union can safely steal the horse, while the small Union cannot look over the hedge"[1].

The strikes also emphasized the need for the quick conclusion of negotiations. While the formalization of the conciliation machinery necessarily involves some delay, attempts should be made to speed up the working of the same. Despite the intricacies involved in the drawing up of the Agreements between the Board and the N.A.C.O.D.S., it would not be a rash judgement on the Board to say that the 34 weeks taken in protracted negotiations were far too much.

Summary

It will be idle to suggest that the numerous problems which beset the industry in the realm of industrial conflict have been touched upon in the course of the discussion of the six disputes. Generalisations are erroneous, more so in the coal industry, where the local and regional differences defy the emergence of a uniform national pattern. The following points, summarized from the above discussion, are presented as constituting important issues bearing on the problem of industrial conflict in the industry:

1. The present anomalous wages-structure is a major source of discontent. While both the Board and the Union have decided to reform it, the task of standardization is not easy to achieve. Objections will be raised by those workers who stand to lose in a uniform wages-structure. But even a drab uniformity, which does not take account of differing local conditions, will not

---

[1] August 22, 1952.

provide the solution. The usefulness of the new wages-structure will depend upon the flexibility with which local variations can be adjusted in an over-all uniform pattern.

2. Technical reorganisation of the industry, which will involve, besides other things, the closing down of uneconomic pits, will, in the absence of counter measures, lead to disputes. Even where the schemes for closure have been arrived at after joint deliberations between the Union and the Board, the persons directly affected have rebelled. A combined effort on the part of the Area and Colliery officials and the local union leaders to explain to the workers involved the need for the step proposed to be taken should precede the actual closure. The Board has a large programme of reorganisation in hand and unless it is handled cautiously and intelligently, an increasing number of disputes may arise because of resistance to reorganisation.

3. The Grimethorpe Dispute, which so rudely shook the respect for National Agreements, demonstrated that the trend towards centralization might force the men to rebel against such agreements and give rise to strains between miners and the management on the one hand, and the rank-and-file and their leaders on the other. A need for devising a way whereby the miner in the pit can be willingly linked up with over-all reforms is imminent. This will mean giving the miner a view on the wider situation of the industry which will help in the smooth execution of the agreements drawn up at higher levels.

4. The immense power which the N.U.M. wields at present has focussed attention largely on the relationship between the Union and the Board. The Deputies' disputes demonstrated that the key position held by the officials makes their disputes important. The need for smooth relations between members of N.U.M. and organisations of other grades of employees and the N.C.B. is therefore important in the interests of industrial peace.

CHAPTER VI

A FIELD INQUIRY

General Remarks and Method of Research

In this chapter we will present the results of inquiries conducted at the spot at two collieries in the South-Western Division of the National Coal Board[1]. A number of other mines were also visited. Though we have focussed our attention mainly on two pits, our analysis has generally benefitted from our trips to different collieries.

There are three main difficulties which an investigator has to overcome in conducting research at British coalfields, *viz.*, (i) estimating the role of past history, (ii) winning the confidence of the miners, and (iii) avoiding confusion in the great diversity of terms used at the coalfields. These we shall presently discuss.

The Role of Past History

First, in no other industry history seems to play such an important part in determining the present attitudes of the workers as in coal-mining. The average age of the working miner is about forty and he has lived through the stormiest periods of the coal industry. Sir Andrew Bryan has described this vividly:

> —— as a boy in his middle years at school his (the miner's) family was not badly off, with an average wage of over five pounds a week. But then came the stoppages of 1920 and 1921; and within a few months wages were cut in half. Yet miners were still abundant; so was coal. In 1923, when our miner was within 2 years of leaving school, the industry produced only four per cent less coal than the record of 1913.

---

[1] For obvious reasons, the names of the collieries have been kept a secret.

> But 1925, the year our miner left school to start work, was a black one. There is no need for me to go into details. I only want you to imagine, if you can, the effect of leaving school to find yourself within six months right in the 1926 stoppage. And as if this were not enough, our young friend has then to face the ten years — adolescence and early manhood — from 1926 to 1936, when approximately one-third of his pals left the industry. Between 1926 and 1936 about 360,000 miners, over and above any new recruits, found other jobs or retired from work. All this was going on while our young man was reaching his physical prime, and I think we can scarcely overestimate the effect that it produced. I am sure that much of the opposition to the entry of foreign workers today and to the recruitment of our miners' own sons can rightly and reasonably be traced to this terrible course of diseducation[1].

The miner thus has lived through all these vicissitudes of the industry and this has had a profound influence on the thinking of the miner and on his approach towards the N.C.B., his own Union leaders and the industrial relations machinery which now exists in the industry. Quite often, even small changes which have some resemblance, real or imaginary, to the actions of the former owners are countered by arguments which would have been apt in the days when "hunger-marches", "soup-kitchens" and "means tests" were in evidence. As an example, we might mention that oftentimes the closing down of a colliery, irrespective of the reasons, is looked upon as a threat likely to cause unemployment. We have already discussed this problem in the previous chapter in connection with the Wern Tarw dispute. No doubt, the nationalised coal industry cannot be completely oblivious of the "human" aspect of the closure of a colliery. Where closure means the death of a thriving community life, it may be better to keep running even an uneconomic pit. But the fact does not seem to be adequately appreciated, certainly not at the lower levels, that closure of a colliery can be inevitable in the reorganisation of an industry on a nation-wide basis. We have seen before that even when employment is provided elsewhere for those who have been rendered idle, the closure of the mine is resisted, not necessarily because the action by

---

[1] Sir Andrew Bryan, *The Coal Miner*, Published by the N.C.B., pp. 3–4.

itself is regarded as undesirable, but because it is considered to be the first of a series of such measures.

We are not making any generalisations here, nor are we passing any judgement on any specific case of the closure of a colliery. Instances can be cited where the workers' grievances in this respect are justified and the Board's policies need a more flexible execution. But the significant fact which needs mention is that on the part of a certain section of the rank and file of the miners, whose number it is difficult to assess, there is no proper appreciation of the changed role of their own organisation and of their employer, the Coal Board, a factor which may be of decisive importance in the successful working of the industrial relations machinery. As we shall try to show later on, amongst the union members there appear to be certain individuals who have very definite views on the affairs of the coal industry and who actively participate in the business of the lodge. The majority, however, does not seem to bother either with what is happening inside their union or with the policies which are being pursued by the Board.

From what has been said above, it becomes clear that in order to understand correctly what has prompted the miners to reply in a certain way to the questions which are put to them, one has to be acquainted with the past history of the coal industry. Questions are not generally answered without the miner drawing extensively upon past history and deriving parallels therefrom. It is here that the task of the investigator becomes both difficult and dangerous — difficult, because he has to sift the relevant material from the mass of historical evidence which the miner presents before him, dangerous, because in this process of sifting he is likely to impose his own ideas and present a picture that may not tally with the one which is in the mind of the miners. The author spent some time in carefully going through the records of the N.U.M. and the N.C.B. and some treatises on the history of the coal industry. Besides, the minutes of the Lodge Committees over a number of years were carefully read. Where records were not complete, efforts were made to fill in the gaps by numerous interviews with officials of the Union, the Board and with the miners.

Winning the Miners' confidence

Connected with the first difficulty mentioned is a second obstacle, the problem of winning the confidence of the miners. This is very important if the conclusions of the research undertaken are to reflect the real situation. From a sociological standpoint, the mining communities are closed societies in which penetration from outside has been slow. The advent of the last war caused some changes when a number of people from the mines joined the armed forces or took up employment in urban industries. In addition, many families from other places were evacuated to the mining areas due to the dangers of war. But this does not seem to have made an appreciable difference and the communities, generally speaking, continue to remain isolated from the outside world. As Prof. Court says: "The mineworkers' ingrained sense of isolation was certainly not removed by wartime conditions; it was in some directions even aggravated"[1]. This was partly caused by the advent of families from outside into the mining areas which helped to "emphasise differences in modes of life, often in a way that left the mining community unpleasantly conscious of being considered socially inferior"[2]. Geographical isolation, to a certain extent, is inherent in the nature of the coal industry, since neither the worker nor the employer is free to choose his own place of work but is governed by geological conditions. In addition, the hazardous nature of the miners' task underground works as a powerful centripetal force that knits the entire community together and gives to it a solidarity which can be compared to that found in agricultural societies and amongst sailors. In addition, the sharing of common past history also helps in promoting this unity during the course of a conflict. Faced with a certain situation, the miner tends to react in a way which is easily understood and accepted by his fellow-workers. The finest manifestation of this solidarity is found following an accident. It is remarkable to note that there have been no cases where volunteers have not offered themselves, even at the risk of their own lives, to help their comrades who are involved in an accident underground.

It is out of our scope to make a detailed sociological analysis

[1] *Op. cit.*, p. 326.
[2] *ibid.*

of the mining communities. That would need a separate study. Suffice it to say that the nature of the mining societies is a closed one, where customs and traditions are still held sacrosanct and handed down from father to son and where the term "mining family" is commonly used, not without a certain sense of pride, to indicate the difference between an "old-hand" and a "new-comer". All this together with the deep sense of inferiority which has been instilled into the miners by the unfavourable course of history, makes an investigator an intruder. It is not surprising, therefore, that the miner is reticent in his conversation with an outsider and does not easily reveal his opinions.

In order to overcome this difficulty the author stayed with a miners' family and travelled extensively in the neighbouring coalfields. Care was taken not only to talk informally to the miners but also to their wives. The latter naturally had very vivid memories of the vicissitudes through which their married lives had passed with the floating fortunes of the industry. It is the housewife who feels the pinch of a cut in wages more than her husband, since she is responsible for drawing up the budget of the family. It was she who, until the time pithead baths were not in existence, had to do hours of washing every day when her husband or sons came back from their work. In families where the male members worked in different shifts, the washing and drying of dirty clothes would be a continuous work. The author held numerous and lengthy conversations with miners, dined with them in their canteens, took showers in their pithead baths, travelled with them in their buses, visited their pubs and went to their youth clubs. The idea, of course, was to enter the community of miners as much as possible, in order to dispel suspicion and to enable the miners to talk freely and candidly. It seemed that the author's foreign nationality was an advantage in this respect. Miners are not generally responsive to inquiries even when these are conducted by their own organisation or the Coal Board. It is sometimes suspicion and sometimes sheer apathy which makes them reserved about such inquiries. The art of the investigator consists in winning their confidence by moving freely with them and in trying to be a part of the life they live and, by personal questioning, to shake off the apathy of the miners and obtain their views on specific problems.

Besides these numerous talks, meetings of consultative and lodge committees, as also a number of disputes during the course of discussion in the disputes committees, were attended, talks were held with officials and non-officials of the lodges and the Coal Board, and where necessary, visits underground were made. All through, an emphasis was laid on informal talks, since it is by these that one obtains a true impression of what the miners think. At previously arranged interviews, their answers are liable to become summary and they do not elaborate upon the large number of minor issues which must form the background for a correct appraisal of the situation. Care was taken to interview managers of the different collieries which were visited. On the Area level, discussions were held with many Labour Officers and records studied in their departments. Miners' Agents were interviewed. On the Divisional level, disputes that were being discussed before the Umpires were attended and the arguments given on both sides were carefully studied. An interview was arranged with the Area President of the N.U.M., and a meeting of their Executive Committee was attended. On the national level, a certain amount of time was spent at the offices of the N.C.B. and the N.U.M., where copious notes were taken and talks were arranged with the officials and other staff of the two organisations. In addition, a few interviews were also granted by the officials of the Ministry of Fuel and Power and the Ministry of Labour and National Service, London.

Diversity of Terms used

We now come to the third difficulty which an investigator has to face. An astonishingly large number of different names are used for describing the same task in different coalfields. Thus, an acquaintance with all these nomenclatures becomes necessary if confusion is to be avoided. It may be pointed out here that the joint committee appointed in 1952 by the N.C.B. and the N.U.M., "to consider the existing wage structure of the industry.. .... so as to achieve a more rational wage structure with greater uniformity in wages and emoluments for similar work and effort",[1] had to contend with the stupendous task of reducing

[1] N.C.B., *Report and Accounts for* 1952, p. 54.

the numerous job-descriptions to more manageable limits. The N.C.B. asked its Divisions to send the list of names of jobs, along with their descriptions, used in the mines within their jurisdiction. The result was a collection of about 6,000 names covering four volumes. A number of different names actually described the same task. After prolonged investigations, the Committee overcame the difficulty by reducing the 6,000 names into about 300 job-descriptions and 20 grades. It decided, for example, that "the term 'ripper' — the man who looks after the roadways — should include the scourer, fault worker, dataller, bottom cutter, caunchman, dinter, brusher, boxholer, kenchman, fettler, and a number of others"[1]. Care was taken to avoid confusion in this bewildering diversity of names.

The Questionnaire

Having overcome the above mentioned three difficulties as far as possible, attention was given to the issuing of a questionnaire. Before the questions were formulated, a large number of miners, N.C.B. and N.U.M. officials were consulted. Care was taken to place before them what have been called "Open-End Questions". The utility of such questions has been summed up by Mildred Parten who says: "During the exploratory phases of a survey it is usually necessary to employ questions which give the respondent free latitude in his responses. Only by finding out what aspects of an issue have made an impression on people and what words the public uses to express its reactions can intelligent planning of categorized questions proceed"[2]. Thus such wide questions were directed to the miners as: Has nationalisation come up to your expectations? Or: Do you think that after nationalisation there has been a change in the attitude of the management towards you? Or again: How do you see your Union after nationalisation? The managers were asked questions on the following lines: How does your present role compare with your employment under private ownership? Or: How do you feel about the present attitude of the workers? Or again: Do you think you have a contribution to make in the nationalised

---

[1] *The Times*, November 25, 1952.
[2] *Surveys, Polls and Samples*, Harper & Bros., New York, 1950, p. 182.

industry? What are the difficulties you encounter in this respect? The motive in keeping these questions vague and of very wide scope was, as has already been said, to make those interviewed talk at great lengths, not on any specified subjects but on all those problems which had been weighing on their minds. This helped the investigator to discover the problems which were most pressing and which were engaging the attention of those concerned in the actual day-to-day running of the industry. After that, an attempt was made to select the issues which directly, or not very distantly, converged on the problem of labour relations and conflict.

In the preparation and distribution of the questionnaire, two things were kept in view. First, the questions were kept direct and clear. No doubt, it would have been possible to make the questions more comprehensive and to allow the miners to reply in details rather than sum up their responses in "Yes" or "No". But it was thought that the detailed questionnaire would make it more confusing. The low level of schooling of the miners in general does not permit the asking of more difficult and indirectly worded questions. Further, it was made abundantly clear orally that wherever the miner found it difficult to understand what the questions meant, he should consult the author and only then write down his answers. The small percentage in the "Doubtful" column suggests that the questions were understood well before they were answered. The idea of having answers in "Yes" or "No" was to make a quantitative analysis of the results easier to compile without giving a distorted picture. Secondly, an attempt was made to distribute the questionnaires to as many grades of workers as possible but only to those who were members of the N.U.M. Thus fitters, colliers, labourers, repairers, surface workers, masons, haulage drivers, cleaners all were given the questionnaire to complete. This was done with a view to obtaining a cross-section of opinion. Care was also taken to include juvenile workers who had recently joined the industry. There appears to be a mistrust amongst the older miners towards the new entrants in the industry, a mistrust which results in regarding the younger elements as a weakening, rather than a strengthening, influence on the trade union movement in the coal industry. We shall return to this problem later on. In order to ascertain whether there was a difference in approach between the views of the older workers and those of new entrants, a column was inserted at the bottom of the questionnaire asking for the age of the worker.

A final consideration remains. It may be asked: what is the usefulness of a survey that covers only such a small number of workers as 116 out of a total manpower of over 700,000 persons employed in the coal industry? Needless to say, the results of this survey are not considered to be conclusive in the sense that they do not leave scope for further investigations. A research intended to have an air of finality on the problem of industrial relations and conflict in the coal industry would have to be carried out on a much vaster scale than the one attempted here by the author. For exploring exhaustively the diverse facets of the problem, a whole team of social scientists will be needed comprising of experts on industrial relations, industrial sociologists, economists, industrial psychologists and mining engineers, all working in unison for a number of years and covering a much larger area than the one covered in the present survey. Such a survey being outside his capabilities, the individual researcher can select a small area and explore the problem with thoroughness and precision, that is to say, as much precision as is possible in social research without the possibility of experimentation and observation under controlled conditions. Social research is a continuous and cumulative process to which the investigator contributes his findings and thus makes the task easier for those who come after him. Thus on the one hand, such surveys provide an auxiliary for the execution of researches on a wider scale which would cover, in this particular case, the whole of the British coal industry, and on the other hand, they help to clarify the minor problems which cannot generally receive the same attention in a macro-survey[1].

[1] For some other advantages inherent in individual research, we quote from two sources: "..... It is assumed with good historical reason that basic innovations in social science rarely may be expected from large-scale projects in consequence of their extensive operations; usually initiation of such projects has been stimulated by the product of some previous innovator working on a modest scale. There seems to be no alternative to continued dependence on the lone worker for new ideas and pioneering studies". (Quoted by Wilson Gee in *Social Science Research Methods*, New York, p. 361 from Donald Young "Organization for Research in the Social Sciences",

Tables VII & VIII give the results of the answers received to the questionnaires which were distributed to the workers.

TABLE VII — COLLIERY A

Total number of questionnaires received = 51

Questions	Answers					
	Yes	% of total	No	% of total	Doubtful	% of total
1. Do you think the Consultative Committee is necessary?	50	98.2	1	1.8	—	—
2. Do you think the Consultative Committee works satisfactorily?	26	50.9	25	49.1	—	—
3. Do you think the disputes are settled as quickly as you would like them to be?	16	31.4	35	68.6	—	—
4. Are you satisfied with the way in which the disputes are settled?	28	54.9	20	39.2	3	5.9
5. Do you actively participate in the affairs of the Lodge?	22	43.1	27	52.9	2	4
6. Are you satisfied with the way in which the Lodge guards your interests?	33	64.7	18	35.3	—	—
7. Do you think your complaints find adequate expression before the Management?	25	49.1	26	50.9	—	—
8. Would you advocate strike action more frequently for the settlement of disputes?	9	17.6	42	82.4	—	—
9. Are you in favour of increased mechanisation of the Colliery?	47	92.2	4	7.8	—	—
10. Do you feel that your job is more responsible now than it was under private ownership?	34	66.7	16	31.4	1	1.9

(Social Science Research Council, New York, 1945), mimeographed, pp. 7–8. Allyn A. Young, writing about the limitations of group research says: "..... These limitations are bound up with the fact that effective research is more than mere routine, more than a manufacturing process. The multiplication of research activities and increase of endowments for research will not of themselves afford any assurance that there will be a corresponding increase of our understanding of the economic life of society ..... Successful research, of course, calls for industry and a command of the appropriate technical methods. But if there is to be anything more than mere fact-finding, it calls also for imagination, for the ability to see a problem and to devise hypotheses that are worth testing. Industry fortunately is not an uncommon virtue. Technique may be acquired. But imagination, and especially the kind of imagination that keeps its moorings, is rare. That is one reason why we ought to put our emphasis upon the individual investigator rather than upon a fixed program of research ....." (Allyn A. Young, in Wilson Gee, Editor, "Research in the Social Sciences" (The Macmillan Co. New York, 1929), p. 68.

TABLE VIII — COLLIERY B

Total number of questionnaires received = 65

Questions	Answers					
	Yes	% of total	No	% of total	Doubtful	% of total
1. Do you think the Consultative Committee is necessary?	55	84.6	10	15.4	—	—
2. Do you think the Consultative Committe works satisfactorily?	34	52.3	30	46.2	1	1.5
3. Do you think the disputes are settled as quickly as you would like them to be?	14	21.5	50	77	1	1.5
4. Are you satisfied with the way in which the disputes are settled?	19	29.2	42	64.6	4	6.2
5. Do you actively participate in the affairs of the Lodge?	25	38.4	40	61.6	—	—
6. Are you satisfied with the way in which the Lodge guards your interests?	44	67.7	16	24.6	5	7.7
7. Do you think your complaints find adequate expression before the Management?	33	50.8	28	43	4	6.2
8. Would you advocate strike action more frequently for the settlement of disputes?	22	33.9	42	64.6	1	1.5
9. Are you in favour of increased mechanisation of the Colliery?	51	78.5	14	21.5	—	—
10. Do you feel that your job is more responsible now than it was under private ownership?	40	61.5	21	32.3	4	6.2

We will now analyse the results of Tables VII and VIII under the following four heads: (i) Consultative Committees; (ii) Disputes; (iii) the Lodges; and (iv) General matters.

Consultative Committees

The importance of the consultative committees in the structure of industrial relations in the coal industry needs recognition for two reasons. First, at the pit level the consultative committee provides the meeting ground for the representatives of the Coal Board and the rank-and-file of the workers. If the committee succeeds in establishing the reputation for being a joint body which tries to grapple seriously with the day to day difficulties encountered by the workers, it would mean a great stride forward towards the promotion of harmony between the workers and the management. This is not to say that many consultative committees are not working well, in fact many of them are, but we would like to emphasize that, as revealed by Tables VII and VIII, the workers feel that there is plenty of scope for improvement in their functioning. Secondly, the efficient working of the committee will be reflected in a lesser number of disputes. While describing the consultative machinery in the industry in Chapter II, we have indicated that the consultative committees are the recognized means for the regular consideration of matters concerning the safety, health, welfare, maintenance of technical efficiency and other subjects of mutual interest to the workers and the management. Thus it would be seen that the efficient working of these committees would show itself in reduced number of disputes which originate from the above-mentioned causes.

Tables VII and VIII indicate that an overwhelming majority of the miners, ranging from 84.6% in the latter to 98.2% in the former, regard the consultative committee as a vital body. It is, however, significant to note that in answer to the second question concerning the working of the committee, there is a substantial minority of 49.1% in colliery A and 46.2% in colliery B who think that the consultative committee does not function satisfactorily. They expressed one main line of argument. As we have shown in Chapter II, questions of wages, payments, terms and conditions of employment do not fall within the scope of the consultative committees. This gives to the miners a certain sense of despondency. Wages, naturally, are the first concern of the miner, and the fact that he cannot bring matters concerning wages before this committee hardly helps to better his feelings towards it. Coupled with this, the constant discussions about the ways for increasing production seem to give the miners the impression that the consultative committee has been set-up to extract more work from them without giving them a control over the amount of wages which they receive in return. The question arises here: will the formation of committees which combine the functions of a consultative body and also conduct negotiations on wages and conditions of employment solve the problem? The answer most probably will be in the negative. For, it is clear that bargaining about wages, which involves conflicting interests, will bring party spirit into the discussions and create dissensions in any such committee. These differences would also pollute the spirit and defeat the aims and objects of consultation. In the present set-up, however, the same difficulty arises in a different way. During the course of investigations the impression was gained that a select minority of the miners were actively interested in the functioning of the lodge and they were also the people who represented the miners on many of the joint bodies which exist in the industry. We will return to this point later when we discuss the working of the lodges at the two pits. It is enough to state here that it is not uncommon to find more or less the same people representing the workers on the consultative committees and also negotiating about wages on behalf of the miners. The conclusion, therefore, seems inescapable that unless there is a profound change in the attitudes of those taking part in consultation, the usefulness of the consultative committees would be greatly jeopardised. The fruitfulness of consultation depends more on the attitudes of the participants than on the constitutional structure of the committee.

The advisory character of the consultative committee implies that it is a body where the workers' representatives take part in discussions and offer suggestions for improvements in the working of the colliery. But it rests with the manager, in theory at least, to accept or reject these suggestions. If he accepts them and the decisions are adequately conveyed to the miners, they then feel a certain amount of responsibility to carry out the policies in whose shaping their own suggestions have contributed. But if the suggestions offered by the workers are rejected, or accepted but not carried out, the workers immediately fit this action into their own scheme of thought and regard this as a proof that the committee does not genuinely try to do what it professes. At bottom, the problem is connected with the more fundamental question of whether the nationalised industries should continue with the principle of workers' participation or move towards workers' control. As mentioned earlier somewhere, the N.U.M. at the time of nationalisation reconciled itself to the idea of workers' participation. The Union decided to remain outside the Board and to continue to protect the workers' interests. Some trade unionists, however, were appointed to the National Coal Board and it was expected that they would treat the miners' case sympathetically, besides bringing their own knowledge and experience of labour matters to the aid of the Coal Board. We do not want to go into the details of this problem here. Suffice it to say that there is substantial evidence of co-operation between the N.U.M. and the N.C.B. at the national level. But that alone is not sufficient. The spirit of co-operation has to seep down to the lowest level, or more correctly, co-operation on the national level should mark the culmination of a true spirit of consultation which should originate at the pits. This spirit cannot be infused among the miners unless the suspicion is removed that the consultative committee is a mere body, where the manager politely but resolutely maintains his own policy without overmuch considering the views of the workers. The feeling that a policy has been imposed from above without prior consultation with the workers is likely to breed discontent. In our enquiry, we found that the significant feature was that even those workers who were members of the consultative committee, and who were generally more active and responsible than the other workers, while applauding the purpose and existence of the committee, immediately added the rider "But, of course, our powers are limited". There seems to us to be a danger of this feeling of helplessness becoming deep-seated and showing itself in increasing indifference to the actions of the consultative committees.

One of the important problems with which the Coal Board is concerned is the raising of the technical level of the industry. It will have to face — in fact it is already facing — a resistance to the introduction of technical innovations. In one of the mines which the author visited, a panzer was being fitted underground, and, though it involved change in the methods of work, it was quite obvious that the new equipment would have lightened the workers' tasks. However, the introduction of the new machinery was being resisted. Numerous such instances can be found throughout the country where attempts are being made to end obsolete methods of cutting coal. This difficulty can be overcome if before the installation of the new machinery, the workers are consulted and taken into confidence. Any technical innovation or a change initiated in the organisation of the colliery is likely to create discontent unless it is preceded by an explanation to the workers of the significance of the change and by convincing them that the change to be introduced would facilitate their work and lead to an increase in production, and, possibly, in their wages. In offering this resistance to change, the miners are no different from the workers in other industries. It is, therefore, all the more surprising that, as shown in Tables VII and VIII, increased mechanisation is not opposed by the workers. In fact, an overwhelming majority of the workers, *viz.*, 92.2% in Colliery A and 78.5% in colliery B, were in favour of introducing increased mechanisation in their pits. The minority, constituting 7.8% and 21.5% in collieries A and B respectively, did not favour increased mechanisation mainly because they thought that the step would create unemployment. Those who feared the return of unemployment as a consequence of mechanisation also mentioned two other contributory factors. First, and the most often quoted, was the fear of an impending American depression; the second was the fear of the increasing intensification of competition in coal in international markets. One miner also thought that the development of atomic energy might supersede the usefulness of coal as a substance for producing power[1]. Most of these fears were expressed vaguely, but they point to the interesting fact that a certain section of the miners tries to keep itself in touch with outside developments. An attempt was made to discover if among those who did not favour increased mechanisation, workers of a higher age group predominated, but on the basis of the data collected no such trend could be seen.

The successful overcoming of the resistance to technical change in the coal industry can possibly be achieved in two ways: first, as we have already pointed out, by a free and frank discussion in the consultative committee of the technique that is to be introduced. Such discussions should be attended by the group of workers who are actually going to be affected by such

---

[1] In this connection it is interesting to note the dwindling importance of coal as a means of producing power. In the United States, for example, in 1900 coal supplied 90% of the total energy demand, in 1945 it supplied only 46%. Coal had lost 51% of its public utility demand, 20% of its railroad demand and 15% of its industrial demand.

Vide Walter Adams (Editor), *The Structure of American Industry*, Macmillan & Co., 1950, Chapter II.

a change. Secondly, this would also call for a more effective system of reporting back by the miners' representatives on the consultative committee to the rank-and-file of workers. Hitherto the process of reporting back does not seem to have been carried out adequately. According to a survey "—— among the 204.... miners formally interviewed, 28% did not vote at the last elections held at their pits; 23% did not know who was their representative on the committee; 43% never saw the minutes, and 25% regarded the whole of the committee's transactions as a waste of time"[1].

There were a few other complaints connected with the working of the consultative committees. Tables VII and VIII show that 50.9% in colliery A and 43% in colliery B think that their complaints are not adequately expressed before the management. This, if it accurately shows the state of affairs, is a serious charge against the efficiency of the miners' representatives sitting on the committee. It is, however, difficult to say if the figures correctly indicate the extent of inadequacy of expression of workers' grievances before the management. Sometimes petty rivalries, sometimes sheer ignorance are responsible for the workers' dissatisfaction in this respect. But whatever be the cause, the effect is the same, for the fact remains that it is not what the worker ought to know or think, but what he actually knows or thinks which is of consequence. A number of workers pointed out that they often found it difficult to pass on their complaints and difficulties to their representatives on the committee, either because the latter were not free or available or because the complainants were tossed around from one person to another. This re-emphasizes the need for effective and closer contact between the workers' representatives sitting on the committee and the large body of the miners. The usefulness of the committee would be invalidated if it reduced itself to a select body and lost touch with the mass of the workers. Sometimes the suggestion was aired that the consultative committee should meet as soon as a complaint arose rather than meet at fortnightly intervals. It was also emphasized by some that the complicated nature of underground work made it imperative that when some problem concerning underground tasks was being discussed, the

[1] The Acton Society Trust, *The Worker's Point of View*, 1952, p. 18.

committee should actually meet at the spot undergound in the pit rather than in the manager's office. One of the workers' representatives on the Committee confided to the author that, even though an underground worker himself, he sometimes forgot or found it difficult to explain accurately the complaints concerning underground work which the workers lodged with him, especially if the grievance was referred to him a week or ten days before the date fixed for the meeting of the committee. It is difficult to say how far these suggestions could be put into practice, but it may be advisable to try them where they do not considerably upset the routine work of the colliery. Another complaint voiced by the workers, which might become serious if allowed to go unchecked, and which was specially heard at colliery A, was that the manager and representatives of deputies and other officials were not active in putting forward suggestions in the meetings for improving the day to day conditions in the colliery. While attending a number of meetings of the consultative body, the writer received the impression that those were meetings where complaints were brought forward by the workers and answered by the manager with the help of officials' representatives, a process which necessarily involved the strategy of attack and defence and, to a certain extent, defeated the purpose of consultation. Undoubtedly, the presentation of complaints by the workers and explanations by the managements' side will continue to figure prominently in the proceedings of the consultative committee meetings until there has been a marked improvement in the general condition of the collieries. But the committee would have set itself to an admirable task if the workers and the management would pool together the knowledge they have acquired after long years of work to initiate improvements in the pit. Suggestions born out of this joint effort will have two advantages. First, they will have the advantage of claiming allegiance from both sides of the industry and will not give rise to grumbling that accompanies the acceptance of ideas which drift down from above. Secondly, such suggestions will bring to bear on the problem the first hand experience and intimate knowledge of the parties directly involved in the work and will, therefore, be useful and practical. While more fundamental researches concerning coal and its production should remain the concern of the scientific organisation of the Coal Board, suggestions for the improvement of the day to day methods of work ought to germinate at the pit level. These suggestions will be examined by the consultative committee and where they appear to clash with the over-all interests of the colliery, the committee will have the right to over-rule them. In saying this, we are not adding anything new to the existing constitution of colliery consultative committees which charges them with the task "to initiate effective measures to improve production in close cooperation with the workpeople and the local Trade Union lodge". But what we do wish to stress is the fact that such a state of affairs was not existent in the two collieries which we surveyed. After all, the role of a consultative committee in a nationalised industry will be judged not by the number of complaints it has heard, but by the number of constructive suggestions which have originated out of its discussions.

Disputes

From Tables VII and VIII a very significant feature which stands out is the verdict of 82.4% of workers in colliery A and 64.6% in colliery B against the use of the weapon of strike for the settlement of disputes. The majority at both the collieries thought that disputes could and should be settled through the existing machinery for consultation and conciliation, though, as we have pointed out above, the way in which the machinery works is not regarded satisfactory by the workers. A substantial number of the workers who were interviewed appeared to be exasperated at the frequency of strikes in the industry, and were very insistent in explaining to the author the difficulties which stoppages of work inflicted on them and their families. It is interesting to note, however, that the older section of workers, while generally opposed to strikes, appeared at other times quick in taking recourse to strike action for getting their grievances redressed. This apparently paradoxical situation is not difficult to understand. Having lived through the turbulent periods of 1926 and the 1930s, they realise the value of militancy, but they also maintain fresh memories of the difficulties which came in the wake of stoppages of work. It is, therefore, quite understandable that in the face of a general disapproval of the use of the weapon of strike, strikes continue to remain frequent. Another factor which contributes towards the frequency of strikes is the delay in the settlement of disputes. 68.6% in colliery A and 77% in colliery B thought that the disputes were not settled as expeditiously as they would have liked. The formalization of the negotiating machinery, involving a number of stages through which the dispute has to pass before settlement, makes quick reconciliation difficult. We have already seen in Chapter III that the overwhelming majority of disputes deteriorate into a stoppage or a "go-slow" without completely exhausting the possibilities of peaceful settlement provided by the conciliation and consultative machinery in the industry. Our contention, that the workers' hesitancy to submit the disputes for conciliation is generally caused by the delay involved in settlement, thus found confirmation in our field investigations. Only 31.4% in colliery A and 21.5% in colliery B thought that the disputes were settled as quickly as they had wished. In colliery A, 54.9% workers were, and 39.2% were not satisfied with the way in which the disputes were settled; in colliery B only 29.2% were, and the majority constituting 64.6% were not satisfied with the results of settlement.

We need not devote any more attention to disputes here since we have already discussed the problem at length in earlier chapters. But a problem which we have not considered so far is the role of labour officers in building up peaceful relations at the pits. This problem needs examination for another reason. Much was expected from the Coal Board's plan in the early years of nationalisation to appoint labour officers with trade union background under the Divisional Labour Directors. The purpose, evidently, in selecting such men was to give to the miners a feeling of confidence in the representatives of the management. However, it appears that the plan has not had the same results as were expected. It is difficult to generalize about the attitude of miners towards the labour officers, since much depends upon the tact and intelligence of the individual labour officer which he brings to bear on a dispute and on the extent to which he is capable of maintaining his good old relations with his former comrades[1]. Despite this

[1] For some examples, see *Manchester Guardian*, August 23, 1954, article on "Miners and Management".

reservation, certain general observations can be made. First, there appears to be a great deal of mistrust among the miners of the labour officers who were formerly members of the N.U.M. The average miner does not seem to have reconciled himself to the idea of one of his comrades crossing over to the other "side" and arguing the case on behalf of the management. Sometimes mistrust of labour officers is openly expressed. During the course of the discussion of a dispute concerning the revision of price-list, which the author attended, the labour officer, who had been a miner himself for a long time before he took up his appointment with the Board, was branded by the spokesman of the miners as having turned into a "Churchillian Socialist" who had forgotten the interests of the miners. Secondly, these labour officers sometimes do not fit in very well with the production and management side of the industry. The production managers tend to regard them as responsible for increased costs without a corresponding return in the shape of higher productivity. Thirdly, it is also alleged that their trade union background has not made them efficient administrators. However, despite these criticisms, the fact must not be forgotten that in the early years of transition when the industry came into public ownership, it was absolutely essential to have chosen labour officers with trade union background. The other alternative, that is, of choosing labour officers from outside the industry, could have proved to be calamitous. For, the role of labour officers in coal-mining does not only call for a knowledge and experience of labour matters, it also requires an intimate knowledge of the underground conditions, which is born out of long association with the industry. In future, it might be worth while to select labour officers from outside also who bring with them a sympathetic understanding of the workers' viewpoint and also infuse a new spirit in industrial relations in the industry. In short, trade union background should be one of the qualifications, though not the only one, for appointing labour officers.

The Lodge

The lodge is the local branch of the union and is the lowest unit in the structure of the N.U.M. The one thing which is significant in Tables VII and VIII is the fact that in both the collieries the majority of miners, 52.9 % in colliery A and 61.6 % in colliery B, do not actively participate in the business of the lodge. This naturally leaves the field open for a tiny section of the workers to control and run the affairs of the local branch of the union. Although democratic in its constitution, the emergence of a very well-informed section in the lodge leading the rank-and-file of workers, who are indifferent and apathetic to the activities of the local branch, presents a real danger. Looking through the minutes of the lodge meetings over a number of years, we found that in discussions, in putting forward suggestions and among those who attend the meetings, the same names occur over and over again. It was significant to find during discussions the great difference which existed in the knowledge between those who actively participated in the affairs of the lodge and the rank-and-file of the workers about the coal industry and other problems in general. Apathy and indifference seemed to be particularly marked among the juvenile workers. The reason for this lies partly in the age-pattern of the workers in the mining industry, which brings about a divergence in outlook between those who have, as we have mentioned before, lived through the periods of the general strike and the depression era, and those who have recently joined the industry, and, therefore, look upon the present level of wages and conditions of work as something normal, and not the result of a long and incessant struggle waged against the private colliery owners — a factor which seems to be of decisive importance in determining the attitudes of older workers. It is this difference in outlook which makes the latter look upon the juveniles as a weakening influence upon the trade union. Despite an inactive majority, it is interesting to note that the majority of workers — 64.7 % in colliery A and 67.7 % in colliery B — considered that their interests were properly guarded by the lodge. However, the minority of 35.3 % in colliery A and 24.6 % in colliery B did not show enough confidence in the local union's leadership. It may be pointed out that much of this lack of confidence seemed to have been caused by petty squabbles and jealousies which are likely to exist in such organisations. A number of lodge officials complained of the apathy among the members, and, when asked about it, pointed out that the average worker was interested and felt obliged to come to the lodge only when some problem arose in which he was personally involved. But deeper than this, the cause seems to lie in the shrinkage of functions of the lodge after nationalisation. While the lodge still continues to play the role of the watch-dog on the interests of its members at the local level, a number of its functions are now being directly taken over at the divisional and the national levels. This is perhaps inevitable in any scheme of reorganisation where the goal is greater uniformity and standardization of wages, working conditions, etc. In addition to this, some people felt that the hold of the lodge over its members had weakened because of the existence of consultative committees, since it was to the latter and not to the lodge that the worker was expected to forward his grievances in the first instance.

Connected with the problem of the functions of the lodge is the changing character of the subjects which are being discussed in the lodge meetings. On an examination of the minutes of the lodge committees at the two collieries, it appeared that the change in the nature of subjects discussed at the meetings was caused by two factors. First, a number of problems which were of pressing importance during the pre-nationalisation days are now conspicuous by their absence; conversely, a number of new problems have arisen. A few examples can be cited in support of this statement. Before the war, one of the important points of discussion was the problem of unemployment, a phenomenon which is at present non-existent. Prior to nationalisation, non-unionism, vigilance committees and abolition of means tests often figured in discussions of the lodge meetings. Thus, in 1941 while discussing the problem of "colliery and non-unionism" at a meeting of colliery A, the minutes recorded as follows: "Our resolution of the nonparticipance on the Production Committees unless non-unionism should be discussed was carried". The summary of the speech of the President of the South Wales Miners' Federation to a conference held on August 24, 1938, contained the following sentence:

> "When examination is made of the conflicts in the South Wales coalfield over a period of many years, it is found that the large majority of them have arisen from non-unionism, company unionism and disputes with unions competing for members against our union. In addition,

> practically all the violent happenings which have brought physical damage to our members, and the imprisonment of hundreds of them, have occurred in non-union disputes and not in disputes with the owners over questions of wages and conditions".

After nationalisation, however, greater time is being devoted to discussions of welfare activities like problems of housing, hospital facilities, conditions in the pit and examiners' reports about them, internal problems of organisation of the union, canteens, pithead bath arrangements, price lists, safety arrangements, occupational diseases like pneumoconiosis, boys' clubs, ambulance competitions, pension schemes, etc. While the absence of discussions about unemployment only reflects the shift that has taken place in the over-all economy of Britain, the change-over from subjects like non-unionism and vigilance committees to welfare activities points to the new and more constructive role which the trade union is now called upon to play.

The relationship of the lodge to its members and to the Divisional and the National levels has undergone a more fundamental change, a change which was a necessary accompaniment of nationalisation. The trade union in the mining industry prior to nationalisation was wedded to the ideal of getting its grievances settled through militant action. A consistently unkind policy that was made possible by some extraneous factors like the existence of unemployment on a large scale, had been pursued by the private owners of coal mines, and though the record was not always black, it was far from desirable. It is, therefore, no wonder that the trade union organisation had to fight its way through, not merely for getting increases in wages and improvement in working conditions and safety, but oftentimes for its very existence. The miners and their leaders look back upon these difficult years with a certain sense of pride. Undoubtedly, continuing to exist in those years must have called for a strong sense of comradeship and a brilliant leadership, with a remarkable capacity for organisation, which could rise above petty interests and devote itself selflessly to serving the interests of the miners. But while all these qualities would be admirable whatever may be the form of the industry, the heavy reliance placed on militancy in the settlement of disputes in a nationalised industry, where comprehensive machinery for the settlement of disputes exists, does not reflect a correct understanding of the role of the trade union. Unfortunately, a certain section of the workers still finds it difficult to leave behind the categories of thinking which developed during the pre-nationalisation days when, sometimes cheap, sometimes genuine, popularity could be gained by giving a strike call. According to our survey, the more militant section did not seem to be considerable, though its influence, as shown in the numerous unofficial stoppages, can be vast.

Under the circumstances to which we have drawn attention in the above paragraph, the task of the lodge and its officials becomes difficult and complicated. Historically, the lodges are the products of the times when the allegiance of the members could be ensured by calling out a strike even when the grounds for it were flimsy, and when a certain amount of recklessness could be harnessed for intensifying the solidarity of the union. The advent of nationalisation, whereby the union was committed to active cooperation with the Coal Board, found the lodges suddenly grappling with the extremely difficult task of trying to infuse a conciliatory spirit among their members. An attitude of mind which is fashioned out of the experiences stretching over a number of years does not easily lend itself to change. While on the national level an extremely cooperative and responsible attitude showed itself immediately after nationalisation, the rank-and-file, or more precisely speaking, a certain section of it, still continues to cling to old methods. This naturally gives rise to strains between the local members and the top leaders and the occasional mistrust of the latter by the former. During the course of conversations with miners, a number of workers thought that the leaders were enjoying themselves in London and were losing touch with the mass of workers. The mistrust among the men is caused partly by sheer ignorance, — a fact which speaks of the deficiency in the channels of communication inside the union, — and partly, as we have said before, by the inability of the miners to re-shape their thoughts and to cast away the set spectacles which they have been used to look through. Perhaps, more fundamentally, it reflects the time lag which generally exists between a changed social situation and the modes of thinking which continue as a hang-over from the past. The reader may be reminded here that we do not imply that the grievances leading to unofficial stoppages are all imaginary. Many of them are genuine complaints and deserve more attention and clear thinking, both on the part of the Coal Board and the N.U.M. But we would like to emphasize the fact that in the minds of a section of the workers the idea exists that the Coal Board is the private employer in disguise, and their own role, therefore, consists in fighting their way through stoppages and other means for wresting more concessions.

Another problem concerning the lodge, which is transitory and mainly organisational in character, is the existence of more than one lodge at one colliery. A certain number of minor frictions are inevitable in such a circumstance. Difficulties arise when a house is allotted to a member of one lodge and the action is resented by the other lodge. The author listened to one such dispute when it was being presented before the Divisional Chairman of the N.U.M. At a particular colliery, there were two lodges in existence with considerable differences in the size of their membership. A member of a smaller lodge, a craftsman, was working as an apprentice for the past two years, but when a permanent vacancy occurred the bigger lodge put forward the claims of one of its own members. Such disputes, however, are bound to continue as long as the organisation of the local lodges is not finalized to suit the changed conditions. This would involve the proper demarcation of boundaries between the activities of the two lodges and, wherever possible, the merger of the two into one single unit.

General

Despite the mistrust and the indifference which exists in the minds of a certain section of workers, the majority of them think that their tasks under nationalisation carry more responsibility than before. In Collieries A and B, 66.7 % and 61.5 % respectively answered in "yes" to question No. 10, while 31.4 % and 32.3 % replied in "No."

The results of this survey would be incomplete without discussing the role of the managers in the new set-up of the coal industry. The managers were not among those to whom the questionnaires were distributed. But, as mentioned earlier, a number of them were interviewed and the results of talks with them were carefully recorded. Nationalisation has brought about a fundamental change in the position of the managers and it would be true to say that most of those interviewed did not appear to have adjusted themselves to the new situation. Most of them showed an extreme caution, sometimes bordering on timidity, particularly while dealing with problems concerning labour. There are two factors responsible for this. First, the great increase in the power of the union seemed to have given most of the managers interviewed the feeling that the Coal Board was heavily biased in favour of the union. This gave them the impression that any policy emanating from their office which brought the wrath of the union was also likely to be looked upon with disfavour by the Board. It was, therefore, no surprise to hear the managers make casual remarks that they had only a rough idea about some problem which was being raised during the course of discussion of disputes. This, really, showed diffidence rather than ignorance, a diffidence which arose out of the uncertainty which the managers felt about their own authority. In this connection it is necessary to make a mention of the tremendous increase in the power and prestige of the N.U.M. The change-over from an economy in which unemployment existed to that of full-employment has contributed greatly in this direction. It is quite clear that even without the nationalisation of the industry, the N.U.M. in a full-employment economy would have been enjoying immense power.

The absence of unemployment and the constant shortage of manpower in the industry has given to the N.U.M. the right of having a virtual closed-shop in the industry. As an example of the great power which the N.U.M. now wields, we may mention the conditions which the Union laid down in consultation with the Board regarding the recruitment of Poles to the industry. During the year 1947 when manpower problem in the industry was very acute, agreement about the recruitment of Polish ex-servicemen was reached between the Board, the Ministry of Labour and National Service and the N.U.M. The conditions laid down were that (i) no Pole should be placed in employment without the agreement of the local branch of the N.U.M.;

(ii) Polish workers must join the N.U.M.; and (iii) in the event of redundancy Polish workers should be the first to go[1].

From the above discussion it is clear that the managers, howsoever much they might dislike the increase in the power of the Union, have to adjust themselves to the changed conditions. It is, therefore, essential that instead of treating the Union as an adversary, they should look upon it as a partner in a common task. "...... given conditions of "full employment"", says Prof. Cole, "the relations between managers and men are bound under any system to be different from what they have been in the past, and that management must adapt itself to the new situation, in which the men no longer go in constant fear of the sack"[2].

Another factor which creates a feeling of uncertainty among the managers is their unclear role in the network of the new official hierarchy that has sprung up with the advent of nationalisation. Under the regime of private ownership the manager had a clear idea of his duties. The only superior he had to look to was the Director of the company which owned the colliery. But in regard to the working of the colliery and its day-to-day affairs, the manager had the supreme authority. But now under the new set-up, wherein the workers' representatives participate increasingly in the running of the industry, the manager finds himself in the dilemma of discussing matters with people whom, previously, he used to order around, and of finding in a field that was entirely his own some other officials whose authority seems to overlap with his own, e.g., the Area Labour Officer. To this change the manager finds it difficult to adjust. Memories, particularly of lost power, are difficult to forget. A manager neatly summed up his own feelings as well as those of some of his colleagues when he said: "The managers are to manage and not to be managed".

Summary

We can now sum up the findings of our field inquiry as follows:

(i) There appears to be a general satisfaction with the structure of the industrial relations machinery in the coal industry. But

[1] N.C.B., *Report and Accounts for* 1947, p. 46.
[2] G. D. H. Cole, *National Coal Board*, Fabian Research Series No. 129, p. 17.

there is a substantial proportion of the workers who think that the utilization of this machinery is not satisfactory. It is also evident that there exists a gulf between a tiny section of the workers who are members of the consultative committee and otherwise also very active and the rank-and-file of the miners. This points to the desirability of bringing the mass of the workers in closer contact with the activities of the consultative committee rather than leave them as disinterested spectators to the activities of a select body.

(ii) Indifference and apathy among the majority of miners towards the affairs of the lodge seem to be fairly widespread, though generally speaking, the workers have confidence in the leadership of the lodge. The cause of this apathy lies partly in the shrinkage of the functions of the lodge after nationalisation, and partly in the view held by a small section of the workers that the comprehensive industrial relations machinery which exists lessens the amount of reliance which the workers place on the lodge. At the same time, the difficulties of the lodge officials should not be underestimated. They have to educate their members, who have battled relentlessly for their rights over a long period, into a more conciliatory approach. On the national level, the union approaches problems in a more responsible way, but the same attitude is not visible at local levels.

(iii) Among the majority of miners there appears to be consciousness of the change that has come about after nationalisation, although they do not seem to be very clear as to how and where this change manifests itself.

(iv) A decisive majority is opposed to the increased adoption of the strike-method for the settlement of disputes. If despite this strikes remain frequent, the reason is to be found in the attitude of a small section of the workers who still hold sacred the weapon of strike and who, because of the attitudes of the miners in general having been formed during the period of intense industrial conflict, find quick response among the workers as a whole.

(v) The managers find it difficult to adjust themselves to the change from private to national ownership. They view with growing fear the increasing power of the union and this, coupled with their unclear role in the new hierarchy, makes them hesitant in taking decisive actions in their own collieries.

GPSR Compliance

The European Union's (EU) General Product Safety Regulation (GPSR) is a set of rules that requires consumer products to be safe and our obligations to ensure this.

If you have any concerns about our products, you can contact us on ProductSafety@springernature.com

In case Publisher is established outside the EU, the EU authorized representative is:

Springer Nature Customer Service Center GmbH
Europaplatz 3
69115 Heidelberg, Germany

Batch number: 10824476

Printed by Printforce, the Netherlands